Alisa, Alice

Dragica Potočnjak

Translated by Lesley Anne Wade

intellect™
Bristol, UK
Portland, OR, USA

First published in the UK in 2003 by
Intellect Books, PO Box 862, Bristol BS99 1DE, UK

First published in the USA in 2003 by
Intellect Books, ISBS, 920 NE 58th Ave. Suite 300, Portland, Oregon 97213-3786, USA

Series Editor: Roberta Mock
Copy Editor: Julie Strudwick
Cover photograph: Sarah Swainson (Copyright © 1998)
Mise-en-scene: Roberta Mock
Cover design: Paul Prudden

A catalogue record for this book is available from the British Library

ISBN 1-84150-104-2

Printed in Great Britain by 4edge Ltd, Hockley. www.4edge.co.uk

Author

Dragica Potočnjak was born 29 May 1958 in Prelog, Croatia. In 1964 her family moved to Ljubljana, Slovenia.

She is a theatre and film actress, a playwright and author and a mentor for acting in the theatre.

In 1981 she completed her studies in acting at the Theatre, Film and Television Academy in Ljubljana. She has been employed as a theatre actress in the Slovensko Mladinsko Gledališče (Slovenian Youth Theatre) since 1981. She was Movie Actress of the Year in Slovenia in 1983.

She founded a theatre group of young Bosnian refugees in Slovenia, Nepopravljivi optimisti (The Incorrigible Optimists), which she led from 1992 to 1996.

She won the second prize for the project Pregnanci (Refugees), as part of the international action 'European Youth Council against Racism, Antisemitism, Xenophobia and Intolerance', Eurovision, the European Prize, Tampere, Finland, in 1994.

THEATRE PIECES

Slepe miši (Blind Mice), Slovensko Mladinsko Gledališče (The Slovenian Youth Theatre), Ljubljana, 1996.
Metuljev ples (Butterfly Dance), Slovensko Narodno Gledališče (The Slovenian National Theatre), Ljubljana, 1996.
Alisa, Alica (Alisa, Alice), Slovensko Ljudsko Gledališče (The Slovenian Public Theatre), Celje, January 2000; awarded the Golden Lion at the International Festival of Small and Experimental Stages in Umag, Croatia, 2001.
Kalea, Roma Theatre Pralipe, Mullheim, Germany with the Theatre des Augenblicks, Festival – Context Europe 2002, Vienna, Austria, October 2002.

The above four dramas were all nominated for the Grum Award, the highest Slovenian award for drama.

Hiša brez strehe (House Without a Roof), 1996. Awarded the Župančičeva nagrada (The City of Ljubljana Prize).
La Noche de Casandra, 2000, with M. P. Daniele, Italy, A. Nascimento, Portugal, M. Visniec, France, M. Morillo, J.P.Heras in R. H. Garrido, Spain; performed at the Teatro de Garcia Lorca, Getafe, Madrid; La Escuela Superior de Cine y Teatro de Lisboa; Teatro Stabile, L'Aquilla, Italy, April 2001.

Hrup, ki ga povzročajo živali, je neznosen (The Noise Animals Cause is Unbearable), Theater im Keller, Graz 2003 Kulturhauptstadt Europas (Cultural Capital of Europe 2003 – Graz); winner of the international competition Unbekannte Nachbarn (Unknown Neighbours), Graz Kulturhauptstadt Europas (Cultural Capital of Europe - Graz), 2003.
Smer zahod (Go West), Cankarjev dom, Ljubljana, March 2003.

Acknowledgements

This book was published with the support of the Trubar Foundation at the Slovene Writers' Association, Ljubljana, Slovenia.

Research for this publication was funded by the Arts and Humanities Research Board.

All quotations in the playtext are from Lewis Carroll's *Alice in Wonderland*.

Author's Preface
Stories from my Shoes

When I am asked why I began to write plays, I invariably reply: 'Because at a certain point in my life I began to have a little more time.' After a fairly successful acting career, descended a dreadful silence.

That is not the whole truth, however, because I have actually been writing dramatic dialogue for as long as I can remember. Even before I learned to write! I began somewhere between the ages of three and seven. The most tender moments of the everyday life of a child contain stories, but, at that time, no one around me seemed to be able to find enough time to tell me any. So I just made them up myself, and, shortly afterwards, began to write them down.

I wrote in my shoes, or, in summer, when I was barefoot, on the grass or sand. At first I think I was a little embarrassed, but then, as with every necessity, I got used to it. For a long time, however, the stories from my shoes remained, for various reasons, my secret. At first I thought that my childhood friends would not be very receptive to them. They also failed to show much understanding when I told them the occasional story orally. They found them too fabricated. But the more fictitious they were, the more I liked them!

I wrote the stories – which mostly took place in dialogue form – with my big toes. When they got tired, my other toes jumped to their assistance; especially the little ones. Writing progressed very quickly until I learned my letters. Then it became much more tiresome, because I had to write each letter separately. All the pleasant, good, courageous and sensible people lived in my right shoe, and in my left, the ugly, filthy, wicked and foolish. (Probably because on paper I also write with my right hand.) Later, after I had learned to write, I remember that many details arose which seemed of life importance. Where did you begin to form a letter, for example, at the top or the bottom? Or should the two letters which I began to write underneath, stand next to each other or not, and so on. Before this, I had written everything in one breath. Now, besides their important content, words had to have a certain form.

Everything went very well until I began school and had to wear shoes that were either too small or too narrow. Highly dramatic stories were taking place in them at that time. As a rule, I finished these with cramp in my left instep. It still hurts me now even to think of it! Difficulties began, as with everything else, (including the activity just described) when I went to school. I became aware of another fact: handwriting and writing things down become very complicated and difficult, even painful, when you actually start learning to write! According to a certain logic, things ought to be just the opposite way around. But then logic is sometimes a very complicated matter. And since paper puts up with all kinds of things, I was pleased when I began to be praised for what I had written on it. From then on my difficulties began in earnest.

I am consoled by the fact that I still cannot wear sandals and open shoes. In fact, I am still afraid someone might notice my surprisingly limber writer's toes rising and falling dramatically and moving hither and thither. My toes also don't like stories which remind them – however vaguely – of my life. They have sworn an oath to put down only fiction.

That is why I have not used them to write this story, even though it would still give me so much pleasure to whisper into your ear that it was written in my right shoe, or rather slipper. I would still like to add that when writing this story my left big toe was continually bothering the right one, even though this is not true. (Namely with the plea: for God's sake let her friend on the right rest a little, for you can see from a distance how tired she is.) Anyway, we all know she wanted the main role in this play to be hers again. And if I may be somewhat frank for a moment and perhaps a little pedantic, I must also confess that my left big toe, the one that describes the dark side of things, is more worn out than the right. But in spite of that, the poor thing still insists on grabbing the limelight.

As if she did not know that that is exactly how all plays begin and end.

Alisa, Alice

Although the immediate context is the exile of a Bosnian refugee in Slovenia, the play is about broader European attitudes towards refugees. Directors may choose to change the specific context.

The action takes place in Magda's living-dining room, from the evening until the following morning.

The furniture is of various styles, predominantly baroque reproductions. The room, though large, gives the impression of being crowded because of the large number of poorly arranged ornaments. Vases are choked with every possible variety of flower, particularly dried ones; goblin tapestries, pictures and photographs in old, heavy frames cover the walls. There is an over-abundance of gilt, crystal and porcelain. The covers and cushions on the sofa are colour co-ordinated with the red velvet carpet and curtains. At least the red velvet is of a shade that, next to the gold, somehow saves the room from complete incongruity, providing a gentle breath of elegance that helps to create a feeling of harmony.

When Alisa is trying to annoy Magda, or to get revenge, she speaks with deliberately poor grammar and a strong accent, and adds some Bosnian words.

The Characters

Alisa (a seventeen year-old refugee from somewhere else)

Magda (a fifty year-old office worker)

Irena (a forty-five-year-old, Magda's friend)

Leo (a fifty-five-year-old, Irena's husband)

Vladimir (a fifty year-old, Magda's husband)

Alisa, Alice

Act One

A festively decorated table for two has been laid in the large living-dining room. ALISA is singing barely audibly what to our ears is a foreign sounding melody, full of feeling, tense, deep (we will hear the same melody again at the end). She makes the final adjustments to the table, then sits there and pulls a notebook out of one pocket and a packet of tablets from the other. She searches through her notebook for the words she needs.

ALISA
(*Reading from her notebook, quoting.*) 'I invite you to Alice's dinner party this afternoon.' Afternoon? No, evening. Evening dinner party. Yes! (*Reading again, quoting.*) 'I didn't know I was to have a party at all', said Alice, 'but if there is to be one, I think I ought to invite the guests.' O.K. No problem about that! Last supper if you want.

(*The phone rings once, twice, three times...ALISA pays no attention to it.*)

(*Reading again, quoting.*) 'Look up, speak nicely, and don't twiddle your fingers all the time.'

(*The telephone continues to ring.*)

(*Shouts.*) Leave me alone, just leave me alone! I'll cut it off!
(*The telephone stops ringing.*)

Prasac! Shithead!

(*She takes out a large number of pills of various colours, placing them one by one onto the plates and into the glasses, sharing them out slowly and carefully. She then proceeds to act out dining. Her behaviour is exaggeratedly 'fancy' and affected, her voice fairly coarse, producing sounds of munching, belching and laughter. She enjoys herself hugely when speaking in an artificial voice, overdoing it a lot, and obviously imitating someone. MAGDA has told her this story several times. She speaks throughout with a strong foreign accent.*)

It happened many times that he came home very late in the evening, you know. And me poor thing I was waiting for him, was waiting and was...And I did not eat. *Uopšte*, I did not. I was not starving, not at all, *razumiješ ti to*? Can you imagine? But when the hunger started, I knew he is on the way home. And I was not wrong, jer on was already coming up the stairs. The next moment he rang the bell and me full of joy runned into his arms. Kiss! Kiss! *Strašno*! Disgusting! He put down his bag, took off his coat and his shoes...And the fresh towel was already there in the bathroom waiting for him. Every day the same, *kao neki ritual*...like a ritual...Yes? There is something majestic in that! And then a wonderful smell came from the kitchen. Mmmmmmmmm...The most pleasant titillation followed by the most stupefactioned (*Like a dialogue*) – stupefactioned? – no, vaporising – vaporising? – no, *šta me briga*! I don't care. Vapour! No! (*Very depressed.*) I hate it! I'll never learn it. *Neču, neču da učim. Mrzim vas, sve vas mrzim!* I hate you, I hate this...this...everything! No more learning, no more living. No more languages! No more Alisa! Nothing! *Ništa! Ništa!* (*Gestures as though she were going to knock things over on the table, then suddenly stops and slowly calms down.*) Alisa – Alice, you naughty Alice! – Alice? – Yes. – No, no. – Here we go again!

(*Continues speaking as she was before her outburst.*) All the time in the rythm of pleasant and unobtrusive music. *Muzika!* La, la, la, la, la, la... la! The king's smile spread over his slightly swollen and saliva sprinkled lips. Oh, yes! His grateful eyes melted over my fingers, which were serving him this ready-made artificial food with completely unartificial elegance.

(*The telephone rings again.*)

And Vladimir the king, with a small 'k', he was – ooh and aah, and oh – he was sighing and clicking and smacking and licking his lips and he was exerting himself with satisfaction and delight. (*Speaks into the telephone.*) He was delightfuly satisfied, oh, no, satisfactionally delightful! His stomach swelled up like risen bread, so all the buttons of his snow-white shirt bursted and jumped merrily around the kitchen – pok, pok, pok! There. (*Gestures with her hand. Now speaking to the person on the telephone, she changes her voice.*)

Don't you understand? How come you... It's me, I do not understand you. Who? You. *Molim te..ne volim*, I don't want... *molim*. Please...No, not pleased. Please! Just leave me please, not love me, leave me, I've said leave me! *Ostavi me, neču više*! No, no, *ne, rekla sam ne*! I said no! Sad? You are sad? Sad? Who is supposed to be sad here?! Sad?! (*Hangs up.*) Fooey, fooey, fooey...Disgusting!

(*Puts the pills back into their packet during the following.*) And then my little hands lifted him up, pleasant dozy, like this and most carefully leaded him over to couch, where the poor devil fall to sleep. But I happily (and whistlingly) skip off to wash the dishes. I press his leftovers into my mouth. Baaah, baaah...

(*The telephone rings again.*)

(*Very loudly.*) *Prasac! Svinja!*

(*Into the receiver.*) You old pig! Old disgusting pig! I hate you, leave me alone.

I can not do it any more. *Neču*! No more! Fooey! (*Places the receiver on the table.*)

Now all we've got is flowers, only flowers, flowers, stinking wreaths of flowers! (*Deliberately knocking over one of the vases.*)

(*MAGDA enters, carrying a fresh bunch of flowers. ALISA immediately attempts to tidy the vase.*)

MAGDA
(*Shouting.*) Don't touch them!

(*ALISA flinches, stops, does not dare to turn around. She slowly adjusts her clothes and hair.*)

How many times have I told you already, they're not to be touched?!

ALISA
(*Still turned away.*) I did not touch them.

MAGDA
What are you looking for there then?

(*ALISA does not reply.*)

What are you nosing around for?!

ALISA
(*Loudly.*) I, nothing?

MAGDA
No, not nothing. Nosing! You nose around!

ALISA
Nose…my nose…how?

MAGDA
No, not nose, nosing, you're nosing around!

ALISA
(*Turning around and acting in amazement.*) I am not understanding.

MAGDA
What are you saying?!

ALISA
Oh, I am sorry, I do not understand. Nose around – I do not understand this expression. I truly not…

MAGDA
Nose around means you're looking for something where you shouldn't be, amongst foreign, amongst my things.

ALISA
Oh, really?

MAGDA
(*Forcefully.*) Yes! Write it down, so you won't be asking me again.

ALISA
I will write it down. (*She clutches at her pocket.*) I do not know where is my notebook. I will remember it – Nose-a-round. Have you pencil? I will write it on the tablecloth.

MAGDA
My God, what next!? Take these flowers then!

ALISA
Joj, I am sorry, I was afraid to forget the words. (*Quoting.*) 'I can read words of one letter' – only.

MAGDA
Where did you get that from?

ALISA
Oh, I read it somewhere. Before…

(*She takes the flowers out of MAGDA's hands, smells them, pulls a face. She turns to MAGDA.*)

Ooh, what a scent, so beautiful. Are you tired?

MAGDA
They stink. Spray them with perfume! Your pencil's on the writing desk, dumbo.

ALISA
Dumbo. (*She laughs.*) I love that – dumbo.

MAGDA
You don't say you love it, you say you like it. There's a difference.

ALISA
How is that? If I am loving it then I am liking it. Yoy! (*She covers her lips when she realises she has made a linguistic mistake.*)

MAGDA
You're going to have trouble grasping it. It's too much for your brain. Well, go on, correct it now. You must correct your mistakes every time.

ALISA
(*Putting the flowers into a vase on the table.*) No matter what I do I am never going to grasp it…It is too much for my…(*Changes what she was going to say, and indicates her heart.*)

MAGDA
Before that. You don't remember, do you?

ALISA
(*With a smile.*) I do! I said: If I love it then I like it, instead of: If something seems lovely to me, then I also like it.

(*MAGDA does not comment. She throws herself onto the sofa.*)

MAGDA
(*After a while.*) Have you got everything ready?

(*ALISA nods assent. She sits on a chair at the table. She now calmly takes out her notebook from her pocket. She tries to remember words so that she can write them down.*)

The same as yesterday?

(*ALISA nods assent, and goes over to the writing desk for a pencil and dictionary.*)

It was really good yesterday. Especially the meat.

ALISA
But why must I cook the same thing every day?

MAGDA
Because that's his favourite.

ALISA
But when I have to eat it for lunch the next day, it is not good any more. I cannot go on eating the same thing every day. (*She rummages in the dictionary*.) 'Nose, noun…A knack for discovery or understanding (a keen nose for absurdity)'.

MAGDA
The next meaning. Read on.

ALISA
'His wife is always nosing around after him – she tries to find out where he is, what he is doing…'

MAGDA
You obviously understand, that's enough! Tea!

(*ALISA goes off to the kitchen. MAGDA opens her handbag and swigs vigorously from a small bottle*.)

(*Loudly to ALISA*.) It looks like you've forgotten already how hungry you were…

ALISA
(*Returning with a tray, which is laid*.) And naked and barefoot and…I have not, I will be grateful to you to the end of my days. Your tea, madam. (*She serves it skilfully*.)

MAGDA
I hope you really will.

ALISA
I repeat it to myself morning and night, as you told me to. And then I really believe that I have arrived in paradise. Directly – from hell to sky.

MAGDA
We say heaven.

ALISA
We say hea-ven.

MAGDA
If you're lying, that's a sin.

ALISA
Izmoliš – you say one Lord's prayer, and he forgives you, that God of yours is so good.

MAGDA
Stop winding me up, or this is not going to end very nicely.

ALISA
Oh, did you think that it would?

(*A long pause. MAGDA drinks some tea, ALISA rummages through the dictionary.*)

MAGDA
Don't I look good, then?

ALISA
Yes. As always.

MAGDA
You said I looked tired!

ALISA
How could I?

MAGDA
You did! You said it earlier on…

ALISA
Nisam. I would never say something like that.

MAGDA
You did! (*She spills tea over herself.*) This is your fault! It's all your fault!

ALISA
Yes, sorry.

MAGDA
How come you're so nervy?

ALISA
I not, I just repeat words…

MAGDA
You're doing quite well for only seven months here, after all…

ALISA
Sedam months I am here?!

MAGDA
(*Ignores this*.) What's the time?

ALISA
Sedam and…Pardon, fifteen minutes past seven.

MAGDA
All right, still time for a shower. Don't worry, everything will be all right. Pull yourself together.

ALISA
Who says that tea really helps you slim, then?!

MAGDA
Have you ironed my dress?

ALISA
(*Ignoring the question*.) What time will we wait to today? I am so sleepy.

MAGDA
My God, you've still got to do my nails!

ALISA
And perfume flowers and write word down and iron dress and serve up dinner and… And when I allowed to go out? I already learned everything, I do everything you ask. You promise me I would go out…when I know everything…when your husband comes…if not before. But your husband does not come!

MAGDA
Stop it!

ALISA
I don't even know what day it is today; I look out, more people have left their coats off, they will be walk around in short sleeves soon, but you…

MAGDA
(*Apparently calm*.) They're still weeping for you at the station…

ALISA
(*As though leafing through the dictionary.*) What is that word
again…nervous…nose …nose a…?

MAGDA
Yes, nose around! A lot you remember! Nose around is the phrase. Nose around
foreign arses. Or in other words – go whoring. That's what you miss. That's
why you're so nervy.

ALISA
I did never go whoring! *Deset dana sem tražila Emira*, I look ten days for
Emir. *Bez hrane*, without food, without money, without papers…goodbye to
everything, *posle svega*.

MAGDA
Speak my language, please!

ALISA
Yes, madam. Speak my language. Be like me.

MAGDA
Did anyone call? I asked if anyone called?!

(*ALISA mumbles something.*)

I can't hear! Did they? (*Expectantly.*) Did they?

ALISA
No.

MAGDA
They didn't? How do you know they didn't?

ALISA
Well I am here all the time. Night and day I am here.

MAGDA
Here?! (*After a moment, too pleasantly.*) What is this here?

ALISA
This is…

MAGDA
Your home!

ALISA
I could throw myself through the window.

MAGDA
Please do, but what will you achieve by that?

ALISA
And you? What for God's sake do you want from me? (*Quoting*.) 'I'm not a visitor, and I'm not a servant.' Who am I anyway? (*Quoting*.) 'I can't stand this any longer.'

MAGDA
Have you been ransacking the house again? Have you been nosing around after the photograph?

(*Here ALISA actually gets confused for the first time*.)

ALISA
(*Panicking*.) *Ne*, I was not, *ne*, how could you think I would, when…

MAGDA
Admit it, you were nosing around for the photograph! When you promised you'd give me some peace until…

(*MAGDA approaches her threateningly; at the last moment ALISA recalls*.)

ALISA
(*Practically screaming out*.) I was nosing around, I nosed around…for – after – a spider!

MAGDA
What?

ALISA
I nosed around after a spider. When you came in, I was nosing around after a spider! *Da*! That is how it was. A spider…

MAGDA
And where is that spider now?

ALISA
(*Lightly*.) I don't know, it escaped.

MAGDA
What, where was it, among the flowers?

ALISA
Yes. Here among the flowers. That big! Hairy and fat and black!

MAGDA
Stop that! Find it!

ALISA
(*Acting as though she is looking for it.*) You devil, where are you hiding, then? I'm going to find you for sure! Yes, isn't that right? Oh, but it is!

MAGDA
(*Quietly.*) Have you got it then?

ALISA
Yes. No! Oops, escaped again! Aaaah. Now I will! Hop! Here it is.

MAGDA
Kill it, what are you waiting for? Spray it!

ALISA
(*To the spider in her palm.*) Stop biting me, or I will!

MAGDA
Yes, do it now! Kill it!

ALISA
(*Imitating MAGDA.*) 'Suppress him! Pinch him!'

MAGDA
Christ, don't you know I'm allergic to spiders?

ALISA
(*Acts surprised.*) Oh! Really?

MAGDA
Yes, really. (*She climbs onto a chair.*)

ALISA
(*Walking around with the spider in her hand.*) I didn't know.

MAGDA
Well I told you!

ALISA
No! Oh dear!

MAGDA
What is it?!

ALISA
(*Opens her fist*.) I can't, I can't kill it, because there isn't a spider. I made a mistake. Error! Look…

MAGDA
Don't come near me!

ALISA
It is a little leaf from the flowers.

MAGDA
Get away, get away!

ALISA
I squeeze it, crumble it, pinch it into dust. Bloodless. Dead. Dust.
Don't worry, we haven't got a spider, that's why we have ants, small ones, quite tiny. (*Picks one up*.) There, see? Shall I rip its leg off? Shall I squash it?

MAGDA
Yes! How do all these pests get into the house?

ALISA
This one isn't from here. She looks different; climbs different; behaves different; smells different; actually she stinks, and she is very frightened. As if someone hunts her. As if she is running away, running away. (*Gets angry. Quoting*.) 'Give your evidence, or I'll have you executed, whether you are nervous or not. She denies it. That proves her guilt.' There is nothing for you here. Who asked you to come anyway? (*Quoting*.) 'Off with your head!' Out, quick march! (*Throws it out of the window*.)

MAGDA
Stop playacting! I've still got to have a shower. From now on every day you're going to take a damp cloth and wipe the floors and the walls and the ceiling as well. Do you understand?

ALISA
I'm going to hoover everywhere, tidy up, wipe up, wipe off, with instructions, this muck, this disgusting filth, this vermin…(*To MAGDA.*) Is that how you say it? And what devil gave you accommodation rights?! (*Quoting.*) 'You are a very poor speaker. Do you know that!' *Ovdje ne bu stopla*…no alien foot is going to tread on this polished floor, dammit! Cut their heads off! (*Quoting.*) 'Off with his whiskers! Off with her head!' (*Dancing around with a bowl in her hand, swiping at imaginary vermin.*) Ants, spiders, beetles and all other enemies, off with their heads, dammit! Chop, chop, chop!

MAGDA
Watch out, you'll break it!

ALISA
I obediently announce that the floor has been ethnically cleansed. Now we must still only ethnically…Hooray! (*Drops the porcelain bowl onto the floor.*)

MAGDA
My dinner service! You've broken more of it!

ALISA
I didn't mean to, I really didn't…

MAGDA
That's all I get from you, a pile of broken dishes and…Get away! Go away!

ALISA
I will buy other one, I will replace it! I will find job and earn money, everything, I will replace everything…Everything! Forgive me, forgive me, madam…

MAGDA
Buy one? You're going to buy one? This can't be bought. It's a wedding present from my mother! It's the only momento I have from her. It can't be bought.

ALISA
I did not know…excuse me, I did not, I did not know…Forgive me.

MAGDA
Forgive? I'm supposed to forgive you?

ALISA
Yes.

MAGDA

I'm supposed to excuse you; I'm supposed to help you; I'm supposed to comfort you; I'm supposed to feed you; I'm supposed to give you a roof over your head; I'm supposed to wear myself to the bone with kindness…Me, me, me?! What about you? What are you going to do for me, then? What are you going to offer me in return for forgiveness? What? Go on, tell me – what? What can you give me in return for all that I've done, that I'm doing for you, well, what?!

(*ALISA trembles and is silent.*)
(*Continuing after a pause. Walking around her.*) You don't know? You don't know because you've got nothing, you've got nothing, darling. You've got nothing to give, you can only take! That's all you know, take, grab, and steal! How can I forgive you? Some things can't be forgiven! Remember that! Clear it up! And don't ever let me hear you say, or even think, anything like that again.

(*ALISA goes to fetch the broom, MAGDA for some drink from her handbag. The bottle is empty, so she sits on the sofa and watches ALISA, who sweeps up and gathers together the broken pieces.*)

Did you forgive them? Did you or not? And where's the child? Where have you put it? Did you have it or did you abort it? Where is it? You drowned it. Did you throw it in the trash? You wrapped it in cling film and…

ALISA
What do you want?

MAGDA
Me? Nothing.

ALISA
What do you want from me?

MAGDA
You're the one who wants, I'm the one who gives! We've already been through that, darling.

ALISA
Tell me out loud, what do you want from me? Do you dare to?

MAGDA
Stop that shit, that's what I want from you! I want you to be silent and obey me! That's what I want!

ALISA
I know very well why you took me in. But as long as I am alive you will never get it, not as long as I am alive, only when I am dead!

MAGDA
Get out of my sight, I don't want to set eyes on you again! Get lost! How could you? You slut, how can you think such a thing?!

(*ALISA has thrown the shards onto the floor, and is going off towards the door.*) (*Jumping after her.*) You're not going anywhere, you hear! Did you think you'd go just like that, just when things are getting hard for me? You won't, no you won't. Listen to what I'm telling you...Listen to me! Where could you go anyway? Who's going to take you without documents? There is no you, you understand, you don't exist! Nobody leaves me, ever! If he hasn't left me yet, you're not going to either!

(*The women stare each other out.*)

Naked and barefoot you were when I picked you up off the street, I gave you everything, welcomed you as if you were my own daughter, you're mine...mine, mine...

ALISA
*Ovako gola i bosa...*I have never been as naked and barefoot as this! They degraded me with hatred, but you did it with goodness! Thank you, Lady Magda!

MAGDA
The photograph! Don't forget the photograph! If you go, you'll never see it again! I'll burn it! Some day you'll see it...Just wait a little longer, be patient, we're friends...Do you still remember it? Daddy, Mummy, Emir, Zuhra, little Aysa, you...in front of the house...Was Emir the oldest?

ALISA
Nemojte više, please do not any more, please do not torture me any more, *molim vas*, I beg you.

MAGDA
I won't. I'm your friend, I'm fond of you, I'm very fond of you, Vladimir will be fond of you too, you'll see. Now you clear up. We'll wait for him together.

(*ALISA sweeps up the shards of the bowl again.*)

Is there a little sip of anything left anywhere? Go on, give me some! I'll never shout at you again. Look in the cupboard…you know where you've put it. Go on, give me it! No, no, there's got to be some somewhere. (*Starts searching in the cupboards, on the shelves, among the flowers, everywhere.*) He hasn't called? He'll still call, the shit-head. You'll see.

ALISA
Why?

MAGDA
What do you mean, why?

ALISA
Why are you still waiting for him? Why do I have to cook these fancy suppers every day? Why do you sip that, that…tea into you?! (*Carries the shards away.*)

MAGDA
(*Taking some tablets from her handbag.*) Now she wants to brain-wash me! Monkey. She's dark as a monkey!

ALISA
(*Popping her head in.*) Pardon?

MAGDA
Water! (*To herself.*) You can't teach culture to a barbarian, she's an ape!

ALISA
(*Bringing a glass of water.*) Won't that be too many tablets?

MAGDA
No. He can go to hell.

ALISA
Sir also?

MAGDA
Yes, Sir, and you with him! (*Swallows the tablets.*) Tomorrow I'm going to buy you some hair-dye, so you can colour your hair. Lighter.

ALISA
Lighter?

MAGDA
Yes, lighter! You look like a savage.

ALISA
Well, you're dark too.

MAGDA
I've got a light complexion. But you look like a black.

ALISA
I am not going to colour my hair.

MAGDA
Then you won't get any more to eat! And if you haven't done the ironing, there's still time. (*Collects her things and goes towards the door.*)

ALISA
(*Taking away the glass, she starts to exit, then turns in the kitchen doorway.*) Now I remember, there was a call…

MAGDA
What was their voice like?

ALISA
Beautiful. I mean…warm. It was an O.K. voice.

MAGDA
I don't believe he called at all.

ALISA
He didn't then. (*Turns away.*)

MAGDA
And what did he say?

ALISA
Nothing.

MAGDA
What do you mean, nothing?

ALISA
I do not know. Maybe he had nothing to say. This happens – no – keeps on happening, people say something they do not know about because…

MAGDA
Stop philosophising!

ALISA
But those are your own words! I've got them written down in here, there is more…(*Pulls her notebook out of her pocket.*)

MAGDA
Wasn't he at all surprised when he heard your voice?

ALISA
Yes, he was a little.

MAGDA
And?

ALISA
And?

MAGDA
That's what I'm asking you.

ALISA
And me you!

MAGDA
Oof! Did you tell him I wasn't in?

(*ALISA shakes her head from side to side.*)

What do you mean you didn't? Why didn't you?

ALISA
Because…because it wasn't him.

MAGDA
Stop messing me about! Who did you speak with on the phone? Was it a woman's voice?

ALISA
I don't know, maybe…

MAGDA
If it wasn't a he, it must have been her. He's stuck it out a long time, eight months. I really don't know what he saw in her. You'd think the idiot would get sick of just looking at an arse and tits. And at his age it can be dangerous. Those young things want it three times a day every day. He could say no once maybe,

19

but twice…!

ALISA
It wasn't her.

MAGDA
How do you know, you don't even know her. Or do you?

ALISA
It was the wrong number.

MAGDA
The wrong number? Another wrong number?

ALISA
Wrongly, it was the wrong number.

MAGDA
Every day a wrong number! That's so strange! And just when I'm not at home!

ALISA
Really strange; you should report these wrong numbers to the police some time.

MAGDA
If the police come to this house, they'll only find one thing wrong, and that's you! You'd like the police to come to the house and find you, would you, eh?

(*The doorbell. ALISA and MAGDA stop dead.*)

You hear that?

ALISA
I hear it.

(*The doorbell again.*)

MAGDA
He's here. No. Maybe somebody rang the wrong bell.

(*The bell rings again.*)

He's at the door. He's the only one who rings like that. Hard, for a long time. (*Calls out.*) I hear you! You can wait – I've had to! I haven't even had a shower!

(*The bell rings more urgently still.*)

What if it isn't him? But who could it be? My perfume, it's in my handbag…

(*ALISA pulls out a bottle of whisky from the handbag first, then a box of tablets that she puts briskly into her pocket, then everything spills out of the bag.*)

(*Pulling her away.*) Get away! See if everything's ready. Matches, where are the matches…? (*Puts on some perfume; then inspects the table.*) Everything's been moved! What have you done? Tablets. My tablets? And where did this…? You'd better explain this to me. A hair? Another one! Oh, you filth!

ALISA
Idite! Go on, or he will go away!

MAGDA
Check in the kitchen and see that everything's ready. I can change later, he'll wait for me…

(*The doorbell.*)

Coming! (*Walks away, turns again and swallows a tablet.*) Pick things up, hide the bottle! Don't leave your room till I call you! And then speak only when you're spoken to! Understand?! (*Goes to open the door.*)

(*ALISA picks things up. She takes the box of tablets out of her pocket and empties them back into the pocket; however, she puts the empty tablet bottle back into the box and leaves it lying on the table. Next to it she places the empty bottle of whisky. She also sprays the flowers copiously with MAGDA's perfume, and then runs to her room on the other side. A short silence. Voices are heard. First IRENA enters the room, after her LEO and then MAGDA, evidently troubled. IRENA has a bunch of flowers in her hand, LEO is carrying a bottle of cognac. The newcomers are laughing and in a good mood. IRENA sneezes several times.*)

MAGDA
I was in the bathroom…

IRENA
(*To MAGDA.*) Are you wearing a new perfume?

MAGDA
No, why?

LEO
Is Vladimir home?

(*IRENA gives her the flowers and kisses her. She sneezes again.*)

MAGDA
You shouldn't have. How come you two are…? I mean – how are you both?

LEO
Terrific!

IRENA
(*Sneezing.*) Sorry, I don't know what's come over me. Maybe a draught. The others aren't here yet then?

MAGDA
Others?

LEO
So we're the first. There's nothing wrong, is there Magda?

MAGDA
No, of course not. I'm going to get a vase. You two sit down.

IRENA
You did want chrysanthemums, didn't you?

MARY
Chrysanthemums? Oh, yes…They're lovely.

IRENA
Some people like them, but they remind me too much of, of…You know? (*Laughs.*)

LEO
(*Quite good-humouredly.*) You're a bit daft then, aren't you?

IRENA
(*Sharply and quite abruptly.*) I hope you won't complain later when I say something as nice as that to you!

LEO
All right, I get it: cut it out.

IRENA
You did ask for them, didn't you Magda?

MAGDA
Ask for them?

IRENA
I didn't mean it that way, I'm sorry, I talk too much.

LEO
(*To IRENA.*) Congratualtions! Congratulations on finally admitting it.
(*Forced laughter from them all.*)

(*To MAGDA.*) You were going to get a vase.

MAGDA
I see you're both just fine.

LEO
Vladimir's not here yet then?

(*MAGDA exits without replying. IRENA and LEO almost whisper.*)

IRENA
Stop asking her about Vladimir, I've told you they're probably getting divorced!
Somebody said they already are.

LEO
Sure! That's his jacket hanging in the hallway.

IRENA
What if it isn't his? Oh, what do I care! Those two have been getting a divorce
ever since they've been together. He keeps moving out then coming back to her
again, poor Magda.

LEO
Is it because she can't have children, or because he likes young cunts?

IRENA
Eeeergh, you're disgusting!

LEO
That doesn't change the fact that the table's set for two.

IRENA
Strange. (*Picks up the empty bottle and sniffs it*.) Interesting.

LEO
What did you have to drag me here for?

IRENA
If I'm not mistaken, you wanted to see Vladimir! Actually, I don't know how long I'm going to last out, I feel like I'm going to suffocate.

LEO
Funny smell.

IRENA
Magda's perfume. It smells disgusting. (*Looks at the flowers*.) Still collecting that rubbish. They stink. Phoo! (*Sneezes again*.) Come here, take a sniff of this.

LEO
No thanks.

IRENA
Open a window. Isn't she acting strangely!

LEO
If she's consumed the whole bottle, she's holding up pretty well.

IRENA
I'm going to hide the one we've brought.

LEO
I meant the tablets, not the cognac.

IRENA
You're right, take one of those and you're out like a light!

(*LEO opens a window. MAGDA returns just when IRENA is holding the empty bottle of cognac in one hand and the box of tablets in the other*.)

LEO
(*To MAGDA*.) You could sell tickets with a view like this.

MAGDA
No charge to friends. So what brings you two here?

IRENA
Yes, what?! Well, Leo was tired and went to sleep this afternoon as usual…

LEO
And we ate some lunch, tell her. You could swop the recipe, too.

IRENA
I'm really glad you invited us…after such a long time.

LEO
Well, I believe you. What about you, Magda?

MAGDA
(*Sourly, distantly*.) And how are you otherwise?

IRENA
(*Looking at her husband and repeating what he has just said*.) Fine thanks, what about you, Magda?

MAGDA
I'm O.K.!

(*LEO sits at the table. MAGDA doesn't like it*.)

IRENA
You still like roses then? They're lovely.

MAGDA
Shall we open the cognac?

LEO
I'd rather have beer, if that's all right.

IRENA
Nothing for me.

MAGDA
Unfortunately I don't have anything else to drink in the house.

IRENA
Oh really?

MAGDA
Yes.

(*IRENA picks up the empty bottle and fiddles with it. MAGDA quickly puts the box of tablets away into her pocket.*)

LEO
I'll have a cognac then. And one for her too...

IRENA
I said I didn't want any!

LEO
I know, you'd rather be annoying. There's nothing wrong with having a drink, is there Magda?

IRENA
As long as she learns how to stop!

LEO
(*To MAGDA.*) You're still a great gal.

IRENA
Why didn't you call me yourself?

MAGDA
I've got a lot on at work.

IRENA
Yes, she told me when I asked her...

MAGDA
Who?

LEO
(*To IRENA.*) Go on, have a little drink.

MAGDA
And how are you getting on?

IRENA
Matthew's got a girlfriend, Leo stares at the television non-stop, and I...well, you know...

LEO
She just slaves away.

IRENA
Have you started again?! (*To MAGDA.*) What about you two?

MAGDA
Us? Oh, Vladimir and me? Nothing, as usual…You know…

IRENA
Yes, work, home, kids…Sorry, I forgot you haven't got any.

LEO
Where's your television?

IRENA
You're not going to watch television when you're visiting, surely!

LEO
Does Vladimir always work so late? It's almost eight.

MAGDA
Eight?!

IRENA
That girl who cooks and cleans for you, that student, she's foreign, isn't she?

MAGDA
I don't have anybody cooking and cleaning for me.

LEO
Do you really not have a television?

IRENA
I mean the one who phoned instead of you…

MAGDA
I've no idea what you're talking about.

LEO
Then we have a similar difficulty.

IRENA
(*To LEO.*) I'll talk to you later! (*To MAGDA.*) Does she live here in the flat?

LEO
Cheers!

IRENA
What's it like, taking a stranger into your flat?

LEO
(*To IRENA*.) I hope you're not getting any sick ideas into your head!

MAGDA
No one's living with me. You must have been dreaming.

LEO
She gets confused sometimes.

IRENA
I know perfectly well what I'm saying, I'm not mad. Have you or haven't you?

MAGDA
Beer?

IRENA
You don't have a young woman who cleans for you?

LEO
I thought you were happy with our little Maria.

(*IRENA sneezes again*.)

MAGDA
Have you got a cold?

IRENA
No, you know I wouldn't be up and about if I had.

MAGDA
Well, we're all unwell.

LEO
Yes, each in their own way.

IRENA
I'm not unwell at all and I also wasn't dreaming this morning when, when was it, around nine, yes, around nine this morning, some girl called...She didn't introduce herself. She sounded foreign, so I assumed you have her in to clean. Anyway, this girl, she sounded young, she said you were having a party and we were invited. She said there'd be a lot of people, all yours and Vladimir's old

friends, you were at work, you asked her, you gave her the telephone numbers, because you didn't have time, you asked her to call everyone! She suggested I bring you flowers, she reminded me you like chrysanthemums, in case I might have forgotten, I must say I really had, though I know you like roses and...

MAGDA
(*Trying very hard to remain calm.*) No one cleans for me, no one lives here and I didn't invite anybody. And I hate chrysanthemums, they're the only flowers I can't stand, you know that very well!

IRENA
Then throw them in the dustbin.

MADGA
I already have.

IRENA
(*Stands up.*) Thank you for everything. Especially the hospitality!

MAGDA
So now you're going to be offended?

IRENA
(*To LEO.*) I'm leaving.

LEO
Women!

IRENA
(*To MAGDA.*) You know what, I was really pleased we were going to see each other. Never mind why we haven't for such a long time!

MAGDA
Perhaps someone had a grudge against you. It does happen.

LEO
(*To IRENA.*) You drink too much, and then...

MAGDA
And how's your son, what's his name again...?

IRENA
I've already told you!

LEO
(*To IRENA.*) Look at our Magda, after all these years, she's still waiting for her love by candlelight.

IRENA
Are you ever going to stop criticising me?

LEO
Don't you know a joke when you hear one!

IRENA
(*To MAGDA.*) We're going, so we don't spoil your romantic evening.

MAGDA
Well, it's nice to have had a chat again, isn't it?

IRENA
(*To LEO.*) Just tell me how this girl on the phone knew we know each other?

LEO
That's a question for Sherlock Holmes.

MAGDA
Some people do nothing but interfere in other people's business. And there's a lot of them around, as you probably know.

IRENA
(*To LEO.*) Let's go. I feel like I'm banging my head against a wall.

(*A door is heard slamming somewhere in the flat. They all stop dead and listen for a moment.*)

MAGDA
(*Improvising.*) There's a draught somewhere.

IRENA
I'm sure the telephone company's got a record of who calls, or at least where they called from.

LEO
Irena!

IRENA
What? What if they've carried off half your possessions while you've been

here? Will you piss about with me then too! If you had anything in your trousers, you'd already have called the police! This can't be a coincidence. I'm sure there's something behind it.

MAGDA
What if somebody else was inviting you? Some good friend...?

LEO
Who's having a good time now instead of us, when we're the ones who should be.

IRENA
It was a woman's voice, young, couldn't have been more than twenty.

MAGDA
A friend of yours then...

IRENA
I haven't got a friend that young. And I know Matthew's girlfriend's voice...Leo!

LEO
Look, I haven't got a girlfriend!

MAGDA
(*Pleased.*) You never know what's round the corner.

(*The door again.*)

I'll close the window.

IRENA
This is just too much for one evening! It all seems impossible!

LEO
Stop acting like a lunatic! You know everything about me. You've got such control over me I'd have to be a flea to hide from you.

IRENA
You could always find an opportunity.

LEO
Is this self-criticism? (*He takes a cigarette from a box set out on the table.*)

IRENA
If you light up now, we're definitely finished! I'm not traipsing about with you to all the doctors!

MAGDA
(*To LEO.*) Go ahead and smoke.

IRENA
With cancer of the lungs?

MAGDA
Oh my God!

LEO
(*To MAGDA.*) I haven't got...

IRENA
You're going to get it though! (*To MAGDA.*) You should hear how he coughs in bed at night, I can't sleep a wink!

LEO
Move to the living room! Stop bugging me for once! (*Smokes.*)

(*MAGDA secretly enjoys their quarrelling.*)

IRENA
You move. But not to my living-room, to hers, if she's got one, of course. Or do you only do it outdoors, then?

LEO
No, in your car, darling!

(*IRENA throws herself into MAGDA's arms, sobbing.*)

You're really sick! Sorry, Magda, say Hi to Vladimir. (*Puts some keys onto the table.*)

MAGDA
How's she going to drive in this state? Drive her home.

IRENA
I'm not going home! I'm not going. I'm not going anywhere!

MAGDA
(*Beginning to panic.*) Come on now! It really isn't anything serious. Everyone sows their wild oats sometimes, you have to take it in your stride. Leo!

LEO
I'm going to a hotel, she's going home!

IRENA
Can I stay with you? I'll sleep on the sofa, please, Magda.

MAGDA
(*Pushing her away roughly.*) Leo, take her away. I've had enough of the two of you, sort it out at home, not in someone else's house!

IRENA
I understand. I'll remember this, don't you worry!

LEO
Sorry, Magda.

IRENA
Now you're apologising to her as well?! (*To MAGDA.*) And you can wipe your arse with the flowers.

(*ALISA appears in the dooway. She is carrying a large cooking-pot, in which she has arranged the chrysanthemums.*)

MAGDA
As pleasant as ever.

LEO
Are you coming?!

MAGDA
(*As though nothing had happened.*) Good night, and keep on being fine.

ALISA
(*Smelling the flowers.*) Someone throws these beautiful flowers in the rubbish.

(*They all turn round in surprise.*)

(*Moves towards the table with the pot of flowers. Loudly and happily.*) *Dobro veče*, good evening everyone, how are you?

MAGDA
Alisa!

ALISA
(*Moves past LEO and IRENA. Her behaviour is now clearly on the border between acting and reality. She performs with ease and with her own kind of elegance. Quoting.*) 'Look up, speak nicely, and don't twiddle your fingers all the time.' Alisa…

IRENA
Wasn't it Alice…?

ALISA
She was from *zemlje čuda*, from Wonderland, but I am from Monsterland.

(*Forced laughter from everyone.*)

LEO
Well I'm Leo, if you…

(*ALISA doesn't even look at him.*)

IRENA
(*After a while.*) And we know each other…from the telephone…?

ALISA
We all know each other in one way or another.

LEO
Witty!

MAGDA
Go to bed now, Alisa. Bed. Do you hear? I said – bed!

ALISA
Yes, that's why I came, to ask you if I may go…

MAGDA
(*Firmly.*) You may go!

ALISA
Why are you being unpleasant? I wait for you to tell me when Sir comes. (*Looks around almost theatrically.*) But it seems he has not. It seems these are your friends. Or are they not friends at all?

IRENA
(*More quietly*.) Who is 'Sir'? Vladimir?

ALISA
(*To LEO*.) *Ali mogli biste biti i vi*. It could be you. (*To MAGDA*.) Couldn't it, madam? They are all the same.

MAGDA
Don't pester people! Bed, I said.

IRENA
(*To LEO*.) I think now's a good time to go, darling?

ALISA
Pester? Pester?

MAGDA
It's in the dictionary. Now go!

ALISA
To the devil?! (*Laughs*.)

LEO
(*To MAGDA*.) Did you say in the dictionary?!

ALISA
Yes. Some things you keep on learning to the end of your life, though you hate them. You live also with some people to the end of your life, though you hate them. (*To LEO*.) Is that right? (*To IRENA*.) Is that not right?

IRENA
No.

LEO
(*With a smile*.) I'd have to think about that.

MAGDA
If you don't go this instant I'll drag you away…I'll carry you away!

ALISA
(*Happily, almost singing*.) Yes, carry me away. Carry me away…Carry me. Carry…

LEO
If you don't do what you're told, I'll just have to carry you off...myself.

ALISA
Go on, make my day...try...

(*When LEO stands up, ALISA suddenly screams.*)

No! No! Leave me alone! Madam Magda!

IRENA
Leo!

LEO
I was only joking...

ALISA
Ali svi bi oni, anyone would think you really wanted to, you want me to...

IRENA
(*To MAGDA.*) Well, this girl just comes right out with it, she has a sharp tongue.

ALISA
(*Puts out her tongue elegantly and acts as though she were removing a hair from her tongue.*) No, it is not sharp, it is full of hair actually!

IRENA
I didn't mean it literally! (*Laughs.*)

ALISA
(*Brazenly.*) Aren't you interested in whose hair it is? It's from...I've got a throat full of them. Aren't you curious? Pity, pity. Oh well, who's interested in anything?

MAGDA
I am, I'm interested in when you're going to shut up!

ALISA
(*After a pause. Speaking and moving in all kinds of ways and tones.*) Today there'll be a dance too. But maybe the police will come first. Before, yes before, but not in time.

(*MAGDA is already pushing her out of the room. ALISA doesn't resist when MAGDA pushes her towards the door, but once at the door she is so determined to say everything that she persists and simply does not budge*.)

(*Talks as fast as possible*.) Pity, isn't it? Such a pity, but the man went too far, you understand? So there's no point, even though it seems like there is, I mean, all there is, is not simple either, but I would still prefer the tiniest, little, little, usual nonsense...In fact I think it is truly better than any sense. But you know, we are always asking ourselves – where is there actually any sense here? And what if there is not any, if it has simply disappeared, if it is hidden, what if there has never been any stupid sense at all? Owwwww, it hurts, my head hurts...Everything will become clear in the end, you will find out everything. But first we must wait for that ending. And then it started all over again. If anyone thinks I'm mad, *neka pita moje*, let them ask my...my...*Oni če poreči*. They will deny it, they will say nothing, they will not move a muscle, because they already know everything – everything. *Neče se ni okrenuti, jer oni več znaju sve – sve...*
*Ostanite tu, nemojte...molim vas, ostanite tu...*Stay with us, do not go away, I beg you not go, stay with us tonight...

LEO
I would, but my wife won't let me. (*Laughs*.)

ALISA
(*Quoting*.) 'What do you suppose is the use of a child without any meaning? Even a joke should have some meaning – and a child's more important than a joke, I hope. You couldn't deny that, even if you tried with both hands. I don't deny things with my hands, Alice objected.'

(*ALISA exits by herself. Silence. They look at each other for a while, they all start to say something at the same time, then they look at each other again*.)

MAGDA
(*Pours a drink*.) Was it her voice?

IRENA
On the phone? Yes.

(*Another pause*.)

That girl's got awful problems with herself.

MAGDA
I've got problems with her!

LEO
Everything she said…

MAGDA
Is mad!

LEO
It seems nonsensical, but behind it there's some hidden…

MAGDA
Sickness!

LEO
No, I'd say fear, fear and sadness.

IRENA
Yes, as though she wanted to tell us something.

MAGDA
Yes, especially that she fancies Leo.

IRENA
(*To MAGDA.*) Don't make stupid suggestions.

LEO
(*To IRENA.*) Thank you.

IRENA
The fact that she phoned us, I mean me, that could mean that…

MAGDA
That she rummages around in the flat when I'm not at home.

IRENA
Obviously it was a big deal to her that we came. It's a real shame you drove her off to bed.

LEO
You've got considerable power over her, haven't you? What's her name again?

MAGDA
Alisa. And she's actually Vladimir's relative – his niece. The daughter of…Vladimir's uncle travelled a lot, a long time ago…after the Second World War. He was an engineer, they built roads down in Bosnia and that's how…he

got a daughter. And Vladimir gained a sister, actually a half sister, Alisa is her daughter and…

IRENA
Don't bother, Magda.

LEO
Leave her, let her tell. I find it interesting.

MAGDA
His brother died.

LEO
Brother?

MAGDA
(*Confused.*) Did I say brother? No, sister, his sister died and…in fact they all died and…The child was left alone and…she was left completely alone and she came to us. Perfectly logical, isn't it?

LEO
Sounds fairly likely. They might even believe you down at the police station.

IRENA
I didn't know he had a sister.

LEO
Half sister.

MAGDA
Half sister, yes. He didn't know either, nobody knew until now. Until everything changed so much down there and the poor child came here. If there hadn't been that – that bloody war, maybe we'd never have found out.

IRENA
But how did she find the two of you?

LEO
With difficulty! (*Laughs.*)

MAGDA
I've asked myself that too.

IRENA
What if she worked everything out, so that…well yes, so that she'd be certain of getting a roof over her head. This would be a good way. You know what things are like these days.

LEO
Even so, she's still an orphan.

IRENA
Anyone would think he's always been such a good Samaritan!

MAGDA
It's a great blow to everyone though, especially me.

IRENA
I can imagine, but you're a real heroine!

LEO
Good joke that business with the uncle, no question, a good joke! Don't you think she even looks a bit like him?

MAGDA
Like who?

LEO
Her uncle Vladimir, of course.

IRENA
Only you could come up with something so intelligent.

MAGDA
You haven't seen him for a long time then…

LEO
It's not important. What's important is my wife has stopped having doubts about me.

IRENA
What makes you think I've stopped?

LEO
Maybe Vladimir won't be hungry…

IRENA
We'll eat at home. You know what she said at the end about there being some kind of meaning…

MAGDA
Complete rambling, of course.

IRENA
I'd take her to a psychiatrist if I were you.

LEO
So she can show him all those hairs on her tongue. (*He laughs*.) That was ace!

MAGDA
Who knows what she's had to live through…

IRENA
(*Enthusiastically*.) She's definitely been raped. Look at all the things they did! Cut off ears, pulled out tongues, killed children in front of their parents' eyes, burned them alive, for nothing, you must have read about it. (*To Magda*) You must have seen it on TV…They raped her, they definitely raped her!

LEO
Yes! There was probably a whole squad of them, a hundred, two hundred, a few thousand. And where's the baby? Where are the children, I ask myself! Look, my hair's standing on end just thinking about all that ravishing those drunken soldiers did to her. Imagine the mucus, the pus, the blood, the punches in the face, the hands grabbing her naked arse and tits, sticking it in her mouth, from behind, she doesn't want it, cow! Bang her against the wall, push a knife into her crotch… !

IRENA
Stop it! Stop it, are you crazy?!

LEO
Yes. Lucky I wasn't one of them, eh?

IRENA
You? What are you talking about?

LEO
I'm joking. How can you even think something like that! I'm not barbaric, believe it or not, I'm a settled, conventional gentleman, who doesn't even dare to fart in the street. We middle-class people do all that secretly, don't we

41

Magda?

IRENA
(*To MAGDA.*) Do you understand what he's going on about?

LEO
Magda understands, she understands everything, don't you Magda?

MAGDA
No.

IRENA
But what you said…that's a really different culture, different…even a different religion. And how old is she?

(*MAGDA shrugs her shoulders.*)

You don't know?

LEO
She has no documents.

MAGDA
Right.

IRENA
So what will you do with her?

LEO
You'll find something! The most important thing is she's fallen into the right hands. Isn't that right, Magda? Magda will know how to look after her, won't you, Magda?

(*MAGDA remains silent.*)

And so we're going to go now.

IRENA
(*Unconvincingly.*) Yes, Magda will know. (*To Magda.*) Bring her over to our place. Well, this has really been…like in a film.

LEO
Yes – where's the dead body?

IRENA
Will you stop!

LEO
I thought we were talking about a film.

(*IRENA is already pulling him by the sleeve.*)

(*To MAGDA.*) You'll keep the flowers then? (*To IRENA.*) She's arranged them quite nicely.

IRENA
Are you trying to screw things up again?

LEO
Darling girl, I won't be risking that again today. I didn't know the girl was so clever.

IRENA
You didn't know? Well, how could you know?

(*Now LEO gets confused and worked up.*)

LEO
That's what I'm saying, I didn't know! How could I know?

IRENA
What are you shouting for?

LEO
I'm not shouting! I meant when she came in with the pot it wasn't obvious – so I didn't know – the girl was so clever. Is it clear now?! Or do I have to go in front of the Grand Inquisition again?

MAGDA
My God, what an outburst!

(*A long silence.*)

LEO
(*Completely calmly, as if nothing had happened.*) Maybe she's even too clever. What do you think, Magda?

IRENA
Yes, she's learned to speak so nicely. How long has she been here then? (*To MAGDA*.) Say Hello to Vladimir if he comes?

LEO
If he comes?!

IRENA
Did I say if? Now I don't know what I'm saying either! (*Grins stupidly*.) When he comes, say Hello to him. (*To LEO*.) Have you got the car keys?

LEO
But I was planning to forget them, so I could come back!

(*MAGDA passes him the keys, which had been left on the table*.)

IRENA
To check if the girl's asleep yet?

LEO
Dead right.

IRENA
We just can't get away from here, we're stuck! We've been leaving for the last hour, from the time we arrived it seems like.

LEO
Maybe we shouldn't be going at all.

IRENA
We shouldn't have come.

MAGDA
I'm quite pleased.

LEO
(*Laughs*.) That we're going…?

IRENA
I hope you don't take him too seriously.

MAGDA
No.

LEO
Pity! Pity!

IRENA
Bring her over to us sometime...

MAGDA
She doesn't want to go out.

IRENA
Really?

LEO
Call me, I'll take her for a walk! (*To IRENA.*) Aren't you going to ask Magda for one of her tablets?

(*When they finally exit through the door, IRENA is laughing too. Immediately afterwards ALISA enters, listens, takes the bottle of cognac from the table. She takes a fist full of tablets from her pocket, which she swallows with the cognac whilst looking nervously behind her towards the hallway. Just as she has managed to swallow the last tablet, MAGDA appears in the doorway. ALISA goes to put the bottle on the shelf. She is using her poor Slovene as a weapon against Magda.*)

ALISA
Nice people.

MAGDA
Shits!

ALISA
It is really wonderful when someone come *i donosi vam cviječe* and bring you flowers. Then you not must buy them yourself...

(*Magda picks up the pot of chrysanthemums and approaches ALISA.*)

MAGDA
I'm going to kill you...

ALISA
Yes, but first thinking, what to do – *šta čete sa* - with dead body? So afterwards they not...what do I know...And your plans with me and your husband? *Ako ovako, kako vi kažete*, if it be the way you said me, looking at things in rational way, anyway it is better not to rush it. Murder in heat of passion! Could be

opportunity missed! Is important to have plan! Plan! You like everything accord to plan! It is shame to break these beautiful pots you got from your mother and these rugs you were gift…when blood soaks in…it would…And so is better, please, not to want to…

MAGDA
I'm going to strangle you!

(*Magda puts the vase back onto the table.*)

ALISA
That is very better…But not best! Best would be little bit of torture before everything else…so we still have little time for prepare, for decide how to do it. And you, you are not your usual murderer! You have consider everything in your life, you have done decisions about all detail, you have take much time, you have plan everything. Then go and kill in blink of eye? No!

MAGDA
You're dead meat!

(*ALISA retreats from MAGDA, hurls cushions at her, raises a chair, they play at cat and mouse around the table. They shout.*)

ALISA
I know! I feel honoured because of that I could experience my death in lovely surroundings of middle-class flat like this, killed by woman's gentle hand, and not there at home by some barbaric dog…Of course I interest in what you do with me after. But you do not know?

MAGDA
(*Grabs a knife from the table.*) I'll send you to hell!

ALISA
But yes, since you already pick up knife, then it is best you use it, I mean, unless you do not want kill me, and then to cut me up into beautiful pieces, *kao svinju*, like pig, you know or chicken or…yes, *polako*, slowly cut me into pieces, and put me into freezer bags, and bags into freezer, so it looks like tender young lamb, then you write date on bags…And every evening you throw one bag into dustbin! Perfect! (*She has managed to take the knife out of MAGDA's hand.*)

MAGDA
(*Pounces on her.*) You won't stop me! You won't trick me out of it!

(ALISA is completely calm. MAGDA hangs on to her, and only realises later that ALISA is no longer defending herself.)

ALISA
I am going to trick you, also because there is always some dog or cat can always find the garbage...who sniffs it out...Well, you know what. The best thing would be to burn everything, send me to sleep with these beautiful memories...ah, but what can you do, some little bone always gets left over...

MAGDA
Shut up!

ALISA
Silence your voice, the bone speaks, through the ages. Go ahead, iron lady!

(MAGDA doesn't know what to do, and hits her. ALISA starts to laugh. Her laughter dies away in the darkness.)

Act Two

The time elapsed on stage has been the same as the interval in the theatre. Music as for the opening of the first act. ALISA and MAGDA are both sitting by the table, or where they were at the end of the first act, on the floor, physically together. ALISA is fairly 'absent', speaking more slowly, though this shouldn't be immediately obvious.

MAGDA
Your suffering wasn't worth it, and neither was mine. Suffering has too low a value for it ever to have an end.

ALISA
Molim? I only pray for…

MAGDA
You go right on praying; I stopped a long time ago. (*After a while, bursting out.*) Why did you tell her to bring me chrysanthemums when you know I don't like them? (*Gets up and goes over to the bunch of flowers that IRENA brought her, and looks at them in disgust.*) They smell like death. I asked you a question!

ALISA
Because of the autumn I can't…Because of the winter I won't see…

MAGDA
You won't see the spring either, if you don't start cooperating! We all pay for our ingratitude in the end! Kindness is an orphan…

ALISA
Until you put a knife in its hand.

MAGDA
What? (*Sharply.*) Why did you say that? What were you thinking about?!

ALISA
You.

MAGDA
Me? Really?

ALISA
Not about you, about my other you.

MAGDA
I don't understand…What you?

ALISA
You…my…home.

MAGDA
(*Visibly pacified. With relief.*) You can't go back again, forget it.

ALISA
Forget? Forgive? You?

MAGDA
Them! Not me! You haven't anything to forgive me for!

ALISA
Only words…The same words…The same fear. Blood…

MAGDA
Stop laying the blame at my door. We've got nothing to do with that tribal warfare of yours. I'm not to blame for anything. Nobody's died because of me!

ALISA
But they will.

MAGDA
What? Do you have any idea what you're drivelling on about? I'm here, here, look at me. How could I have anything to do with that damned shit of yours back there? Nobody's died yet because of me, do you hear? Perhaps somebody has because of you, somebody on the other side. How can you know what's happened on the other side?

ALISA
Only one side is right…

MAGDA
And you're the one who's going to decide which one it is??! Eat your own shit, darling, before you point at someone else's! You just don't realise that you and people like you are bringing your own muck here when we've already got too much of our own.

(*ALISA wants to say something.*)

(*Loses control, and thrashes ALISA with the bunch of flowers so that the blossoms fly everywhere*.) My conscience is clear, do you hear me? Clear! What do you know about my suffering? How do you know yours is worse than mine? We're all the same in the sight of God! And I'm innocent!

(*ALISA has hidden her head in her hands*.)

(*After a while, when she has calmed down a little*.) Clear up that stinking mess! And don't let me see it ever again! You lazy slut, you either stare at me like an idiot, or you babble insolence. That's all you know how to do. And when I'm not here, you snoop, snoop, snoop. You rummage through all my things. You eat my liver, you grind my spleen under your feet!

(*ALISA has picked up the remains of the flowers; she wanders into the kitchen*.)

MAGDA
(*To herself*.) How could she dare to?! Worthless ungrateful thing! (*Louder*) You think you've fallen through a rabbit hole to us? Just so you can act like a smart arse? You can go straight back where you came from!

(*ALISA returns*.)

Do you understand me?

(*ALISA nods assent*.)

And will you remember that?

(*ALISA nods assent*.)

Have you done the ironing?

(*ALISA nods assent*.)

We'll see how well!

ALISA
Can I go to bed? (*After a while*.) Let me go to bed. Please.

MAGDA
No! I want a drink.

(*ALISA hands her the bottle*.)

A glass. That's not mine! This one! Pour it. You have some too.

ALISA
No, I will not.

MAGDA
You will!

(*They look at each other for a while; MAGDA drinks. ALISA takes a glass from the table and pours one for herself.*)

You drink out of a dirty glass, you don't know basic manners, you've no culture, you don't even know how to wash your hands…and still you dare to accuse me! Who gave you that right? What god-given right is that?
Today's been really crazy. When I saw those two I thought I'd have a heart attack! But how do you like what I cooked up for them…They're probably still talking about it! (*Laughs.*) My husband Vladimir, right, is your uncle…his father had a child with your grandmother, your mother's mother, who is therefore Vladimir's half-sister…(*Laughs.*) I like that! Let's drink to that! Your health, niece! Drink it down! (*MAGDA drinks, but ALISA doesn't.*) Pour! What are you trembling for? Don't you like my story? Pity. I thought we might have a good time together for once.
The cognac's excellent though, isn't it? Genuine French. Sometimes they're really stingy, even though they've always been loaded. That's how they got a cottage and two holiday homes, two or three cars, and…

ALISA
A son?

MAGDA
I was hoping you'd given up by now…! (*After a while, and in a different voice.*) Do you know, darling, that this cognac is worth more than your father used to earn in a month? (*Cynically.*) Poor daddy! Was he handsome? Do you ever still think of him?

(*They look at each other. A long silence.*)

ALISA
What if he really did call?

MAGDA
(*Starts.*) Who?

ALISA
(*Sincerely.*) Vladimir.

MAGDA
He called? Tell me!

ALISA
Yes, he called…

MAGDA
And what did he say? Tell me, did he say he's coming?

ALISA
Yes.

MAGDA
When, for God's sake, when?

ALISA
Tomorrow.

MAGDA
I knew it! Tomorrow, then?!

ALISA
Tomorrow and every day. Today he said he's coming tomorrow. Yesterday that he's coming today. Tomorrow he'll say he's coming the day after. In fact he's here every day. But unfortunately, when you're not.

MAGDA
What's this now? You're not drunk, are you? Stop drinking! (*Takes her glass out of her hand*.) Are you trying to tell me Vladimir comes here when I'm not home?

ALISA
Yes.

MAGDA
That's impossible…

ALISA
He's got a key.

MAGDA
I know he's got a key, but…no! Tell me what he looks like, then?

ALISA
He's old.

MAGDA
(*Relaxes and laughs.*) Yes, that's true! Even though he thinks he isn't. But Leo's even older, and you still liked him.

ALISA
He comes too, but after him.

MAGDA
(*Already enjoying herself.*) Watch what you're saying, girl!

ALISA
Dolaze i rade one stvari. They come and do these things. But without blood.

MAGDA
(*Almost gently.*) Well, you're really bored when I'm at work, aren't you?

ALISA
Someone is always here, *jedva da sredim stvari*…I can hardly get things done…

MAGDA
Stop speaking in that language!

ALISA
Why do they all want the same? And when they are old they want them young.

MAGDA
Now you're completely mixed up. Come here so I can give you a hug.

ALISA
No!

MAGDA
No, then! (*Pours herself some more, and drinks.*) All right, Vladimir's got a key, but what about Leo, how does he get in here?

ALISA
By telephone.

MAGDA
What? (*Laughs.*) On the phone?

ALISA
(*Seriously.*) Sometimes he is stopped half way.

MAGDA
Where did you hear about that?

ALISA
Kao da ne znate šta sve ljudi rade…? Why you do not know what people do through the telephone?

MAGDA
Where did you get that from? You've got no newspapers or TV…(*She laughs.*) Does Leo do it to you right over the phone then?

ALISA
Yes.

MAGDA
What's that like, I'd like to know…

ALISA
He doesn't want to do it over the phone any more.

MAGDA
I imagine he doesn't!

ALISA
So now he wants…

MAGDA
(*In a good mood.*) To do it for real?! Oh, the dirty thing! And that's why they came today?

ALISA
(*Only nods assent. As though she were performing a duty that from that moment no longer interests her.*) Can I go to bed now?

MAGDA
No, of course not! Drink a little more, you can tell me some more…
(*ALISA resists.*)

How sweet you are, you should drink more often. Drink! (*Pours for her and puts the glass into her hand.*)

(*ALISA knocks over the glass forcefully*.)

Cognac is drunk slowly, in sips…I'll have to teach you. You hold the glass, it has to be the right one for cognac, this is a lovely one, isn't it? Yes, to make it warm…can you feel it? He gave me them for our fifth anniversary…What are you trembling for? You have to know how to take pleasure in everything, otherwise things are pointless, everything! Anyway, I can't have these expensive drinks in cheap glasses, if I know it's not right …! Look, there's no more in this bottle now either! (*The bottle really is empty. Pulls a box of tablets out of her pocket. Opens the little pill bottle, which is also empty*.)

No, no! It should be full…See if there are any more in the drawer.

(*ALISA walks with some difficulty*.)

I was sure I had some left…Perhaps not, then…I'm getting a bit dizzy. What was it I wanted…? Oh yes! To have such an excessive appreciation of quality…That can be a serious problem, you know. I want, I insist that everything's as it should be! And if it isn't? What am I explaining this to you for? You haven't any feeling for detail anyway. But that's exactly what matters, tiny things, little awarenesses, important details…Are you dizzy?

ALISA
Yes.

MAGDA
Hold on to the cupboard. What if I threw the whole box away at work?! You idiot! Are you ill?

ALISA
Yes.

MAGDA
You shouldn't get ill from such good quality cognac! Perhaps you should go and take a bath? Warm water is calming…Are they there?

ALISA
No.

MAGDA
Not even one?

ALISA
One would not help you anyway.

MAGDA
Who said I needed help?! You've thrown them away! I know it's you. I'm certain.

ALISA
(*After a while, turned away, barely audible.*) Flowers, flowers...

MAGDA
Are you starting again?

ALISA
All dry, all dried up, dead...

MAGDA
(*Toys with the empty bottle of tablets. After a while. With feigned naivety.*) What if one of your family is still alive?

ALISA
(*Still standing by the flowers.*) They only collect dust. Why are not you throwing them away?

MAGDA
You won't get at me like that! You're still hoping one fine day someone will turn up at my door, aren't you? Wouldn't that be nice! And he'll say he's your brother. What's his name again? Emir? Is it Emir? Yes, Emir.

ALISA
Did he really bring you them all? I do not believe it, you bought them yourself.

MAGDA
Of course it's Emir. Horrible name! Yes, if you weren't lying, all the rest of them burned in the house. But what if they didn't? Oh, of course they did! Terrible, that must have been really terrible! I can just imagine how they must have suffered...How they screamed...How they all fried together in the fire. How those innocent little creatures clung onto your father and mother, who were weeping, because they couldn't help them, because nobody could help them, do you ever think about that?!

ALISA
They stink! Some of the blossoms have already fallen to pieces completely, you just touch them and they crumble into dust.

MAGDA
Don't touch them! Think how lucky you were...

ALISA
Brown, grey, black…these are not flowers, they are rubbish.

MAGDA
Not this one! This is my wedding bouquet! I've told you a hundred times.

ALISA
They will not crumble. It is like the leaves are glued on…

MAGDA
But you know they have been!

ALISA
What? I cannot believe it…

MAGDA
No! Alisa! Leave my wedding bouquet, please, leave it. Put it back…Alisa! It was so full my fingers hurt when I held it in my hands…Please, be careful…look what's left of it…

ALISA
And what do you call these flowers?

MAGDA
Lily of the valley, lilies and roses, little white roses, these are the only ones left…

ALISA
Grey, brown, all full of cobwebs! Lily of the valley…?

MAGDA
They've disintegrated into dust, they've gone, but they were…I had them in my hair, I pinned them to the wedding guests' suits, their scent was everywhere, their fragrance wafted…

ALISA
Faded…

MAGDA
Put the bouquet back where it was…I won't mention your family any more, I promise, I won't ever again, but you've got to stop hurting me as well.

(*They look at each other for a long time, then ALISA puts the bouquet back on the shelf.*)

Thank you. Thank you…You see, we know how to cooperate with each other?

(*ALISA doesn't react. They look at each other quite calmly.*)

I gave him everything, desires, dreams, laughter, and little by little he took the laughter away…I was left here with only fear, tears and fear, empty rooms, cold sheets, dead longings…When the tears have gone as well, then you throw yourself into work, you work from morning till night, for years and years the same…You think you're doing it for yourself, but really you're doing it for others, you feel you have to do everything…And so you buy yourself a bunch of flowers that wait with you, looking at you…so that…you can still hope…again. They're waiting with you, so you aren't alone, they get drier and drier, they dry out in your memory…with you.

But tomorrow I'm really going to throw him out. How surprised he'll be, the poor thing! Don't you believe me? Try to believe it. Please, what can I do to make you believe me? What can I do for you to get you to trust me?

(*ALISA remains silent.*)

You don't know? I do. My keys are in my bag. Go and find them and take them.

ALISA
(*Staggers.*) I feel ill…

MAGDA
Of course, if you don't eat anything. I'll do it myself. (*Searches in her handbag.*) We'll make our dinner, we'll eat everything. He can go to hell!

ALISA
I'm not hungry.

MAGDA
You must put on a bit of weight…Where are those keys then…?

ALISA
In the cupboard…

MAGDA
(*Looks there and finds them.*) So they are. Have you already found the photo?

ALISA
No.

MAGDA
You're lying!

ALISA
I'm not lying.

MAGDA
I know exactly where I put it, it was under here…(*Tosses things out of the cupboard*.) Of course it was. No, I moved it. Yes, yes. I know, I know where it is now. I remember…You get the dinner ready and the dresses and I'll bring it to you…

ALISA
Dresses?

MAGDA
Yes, my gold one and yours, we'll light the candles and celebrate our truce!

ALISA
I just want to go to bed, I really feel ill…

MAGDA
Have you forgotten already how you begged me for it? I'll give it to you, really. The dress, quickly, quick!

ALISA
Oh God! (*Sits down on a chair*.)

MAGDA
Your God or mine? (*Laughs*.) And what are you sighing for now?

(*ALISA is still just sitting*.)
All right! I'll get the dinner! Go and get changed! I know where it is, I know where it is…(*Already disappearing from the room*.)

(*ALISA is still just sitting*.)

(*Returns with the photograph in her hand, very pleased*.) Here it is! I've got it! I've found it! Get up, then! I'll give it to you when you've changed! Ha, ha, ha, now I've got you! Now you've got no choice, you'll have to cooperate now, he, he, he! Our little dinner will be on the little table in no time at all now, ho, ho, ho! Alisa, did you hear me? Wake up.

(*ALISA slowly stands up and floats off into the bedroom*.)

(*Brings food to the table. Talks loudly to ALISA at the same time.*) I'm going to tell you what it was like at our wedding…Can you hear me?

(*ALISA responds.*)

The main thing is that my darling future husband said his big – I do! - through his tears and he was kind of sneezing. Of course I thought he was so uncontrollably happy, overcome with emotion…Can you hear me? Hurry up, will you! (*Lights the candles on the table.*) There we are, beautiful! But actually he was allergic and didn't want to admit it, he didn't want to offend me, you know? Can you imagine how much he loved me? Can you imagine that? Allergic to lilies of the valley, whoever heard of that?
Alisa, I'm getting fed up with you! What are you doing?
In fact I've heard they are actually poisonous, but he…if he'd only asked me what kind of flowers I was going to have in my bouquet?! Alisa! Some woman apparently committed suicide with them…Can you imagine? Sometimes, when I look round this room, I can even see how…(*Goes towards the door.*)

(*ALISA enters with MAGDA's burned dress.*)

Well, thank God! But why haven't you changed? (*Takes the dress from her.*) The whole room was filled with them, can you imagine, in every little corner…What's the matter with you? Are you really drunk? Her body was as fragrant as a flower garden, the things people remember! (*She has laid the dress on the chair and already begun to undress, when…*)

ALISA
Madam Magda…

MAGDA
What is it now? Oh no, how? How could you? Ohhh!

ALISA
I didn't mean to, I really didn't…I'm sorry, madam, I don't know how…

MAGDA
My dress! My favourite dress?! How could you, Alisa? How could you?

ALISA
Peglala sam i onda…I was ironing and then I suddenly remembered the dinner and I ran to the kitchen and forgot that…When I got back, it was already…

MAGDA
You're lying, lying, you did it just now, that's why you were gone for so long,

you did it on purpose to get your revenge! My…my dress! (*Walks around the room, presses the dress to her, looks at it, strokes it, sobs.*) Now you've destroyed this too! The most beautiful thing in my wardrobe! Now what can I do…? No other dress has ever suited me as well. I only wore it on special occasions…Now what can I do? You've brought nothing but bad luck into this house. Nothing but bad luck! (*Sits down, her head in her hands.*) And right now, when I'd decided…! Why did you do this, Alisa?! Why did you do this now, now when…It's not good, you shouldn't have, I'd decided, as I'd told you…! No, oh God!

(*A long silence. ALISA doesn't move, MAGDA hides her head in the dress. They remain like this for a long time, each in their own pain.*)

(*Looks up, feels in her pocket and pulls out the photograph, takes some matches, but suddenly reconsiders.*) Handsome, that father of yours, very handsome…You don't look like him at all. Your mother? Well, yes, was she older than him? I'd say she looks a bit tired! Jesus, how many children are there? And they all burned, poor things…One, two, three…six. Ah, is this you then? Look what a pretty girl you were…Lovely little cheeks!

ALISA
Nemojte to raditi, molim vas. Please do not do that, I beg you.

MAGDA
You're a slut, you know that!? How come you didn't die?

ALISA
I will.

MAGDA
Strange, really strange. And there's no one left, only you survived.

ALISA
Emir…*on nije bio tu*, he was not there, when it happened…A man…said that…*da su ga zaklali* …they butchered him. A neighbour.

MAGDA
A neighbour butchered him?

ALISA
No, I do not know.

MAGDA
Oh well, what's past is past. I'm really sorry to have to do this!

ALISA
May I please look at it just once? *Molim vas*? I beg you.

MAGDA
No. Unfortunately not. You could have had it, before…Why did you do this?

ALISA
I do not know.

MAGDA
(*Lights a match and burns the photograph.*) For everything you've destroyed of mine! Now we're even! Owwww! (*Throws the burning photograph to the floor, as she has burned her finger, then runs into the kitchen.*)

(*Meanwhile ALISA picks up the matches and goes over to the flowers; she holds the wedding bouquet in her hands and sets it alight. MAGDA returns with a wet cloth around her fingers, screams and runs towards ALISA, hits the flowers with the cloth, the bouquet scatters over the floor. They both fall to their knees and gather together the ashes and remnants of their memories.*)

Oh, you liar, you rotten liar, you pile of shit. There's not a drop of human dignity in you…look what you've done to me! You whore, if we all spit on you, it's exactly what you deserve! What are you snivelling for? Eat your photograph! What's the point in crying now? You should have thought of it sooner!

ALISA
I could not run so fast…*Nisam mogla…vukao me*…he pulled me behind him, but I just could not, my feet froze in those summer shoes. And had to more quickly, run more quickly across the clearings…I turned round and stopped…I could not go any more, could not go more…I wanted go back, see just once more, just once more…But there was only smoke there…*samo dim*…I could not find his hand, or his…*kao da sam padala u mrak*…so I fell into darkness, crawling slowly through warm, later I understood, bloody pits…There were…smashed up, torn to pieces…He was not he was not…any more…

MAGDA
The neighbour or your brother?

ALISA
Moj brat…Moj…Emiiiir!

MAGDA
(*Picks up the flowers, carries the remainder to the rubbish bin and then we*

62

hear her from the kitchen.) Well, now we both have our memories! Pull yourself together and stop whining! What terrible memories these are, you've got to forget them, we should remember lovely things, not that. Memories like that should be burned!

(*ALISA slowly scrambles to her feet and slowly totters towards the hallway. MAGDA enters when ALISA is just disappearing through the doorway.*)

Have you finally come to your senses?! (*Pulls her back into the room.*) You're not going anywhere.

ALISA
Let me go…I have to…

MAGDA
Dying's the only thing we have to do.

ALISA
I am going to throw up…

MAGDA
No you're not, you're going to lie down, have a rest, you're going to forget about everything, me too…

ALISA
I have to…tell…

MAGDA
There's no need to tell me anything else, because I know about everything…Leo and Irena…You were bored, you nosed around in my things, you found their number and…

ALISA
No, no, no.

MAGDA
I know it's not easy for you, I know you don't like it here, but you can't go back, there's no one there any more, there are other people there now. When Vladimir comes…

(*ALISA is very frightened, MAGDA can hardly calm her.*)

MAGDA
No, no, no, you mustn't think that, I'm not giving you to anybody. I'm your

friend, I'm fond of you, you've no idea how very fond of you I am. I need you as much as you do me, you're my sunshine, my only light...I'll do everything to make you forget those atrocities...I'm going to teach you, I'm going to bring you up well, give you everything I have...You'll see how nice it will be together.

ALISA
No...

MAGDA
Yes. My loneliness has become your loneliness, your soul has spread its roots through my heart...You've got nobody and neither have I. It's as if Vladimir had never existed. Year after year, for the last twenty years, who could stand it? Overnight, just like that, and he never touched me again. Do you know what twenty years is like? For twenty years he's been going to someone else!

ALISA
I did not want...I am going...

MAGDA
I'm not letting you go anywhere! Only you can help me! It's lovely here with me, it's warm in here. I won't do anything horrible to you again, never again, you have to forgive me, forgive me for everything, I didn't want to, I don't know why you think that, even if I did once, perhaps I really did think, but only for a moment, that you could be...that you would be Vladimir's...that! But as God's my witness, God's my witness, I don't think it any more, no, look in front of you, I'm begging His forgiveness, on my knees I'm begging Him!

ALISA
Get up...

(*It is really impossible to tell who is holding up whom.*)

MAGDA
You're not going, are you? (*Kisses her.*)

ALISA
Dress...my...dress?

MAGDA
(*Still dazed by her own speech.*) What dress?

ALISA
My...

MAGDA
You can't be thinking of that rag I found you in in the street?

ALISA
Dress…

MAGDA
I threw it in the dustbin.

(*ALISA would cry out in pain, but suddenly she can't; increasingly, more and more inarticulate sounds come from her*.)

And now you're going to cry again for that stinking rag? I thought I was doing you a favour. Why didn't you remember it before? I know why!

ALISA
Your…(*Starts to undress, slowly and with difficulty. Sits on the floor*.)

MAGDA
What are you doing? What's the matter with you? Have you gone mad? Get dressed!

ALISA
I was naked and barefoot, *gola i bosa, ali ovako nikad*, but never like this, they put me down with hatred, but you do it with love and kindness. God knew, that is why he gave you no children. Carry on, iron lady. And I know, now I know. I am in the sky, on the way to the sky, *nebo do neba*…I am going home, I am going to lie down in the silence…

MAGDA
Of course you are, but you're going to pay me for everything first!

ALISA
(*Undressed, with her last words she lies on the floor like a corpse*.) I am going to forget everything, everything. I am going to bury myself in the earth with my fingers. I will cover myself with earth and forget…

MAGDA
Of course you're going to forget, very soon, because you've obviously gone mad. Well, that's all I needed. Now…(*Laughs*.) Now we've got her, Vladimir! I'll give you a dress! Stop pretending! Do you think I don't know you're pretending, I'll wake you up, don't you worry, you remembered that well enough but you won't, and you'll never…neither will he! (*Shakes her and slaps her cheeks. Pulls her and tries to lift her*.) No one has ever put one over on me

65

yet, and they've been cleverer than you. Not even him, tomorrow first thing he'll be standing there at my door. He's going to lick every one of my fingers a hundred times before I touch him again. We already know his game off by heart! But he won't go anywhere else any more now, now he won't have to go crawling after foreign skirts any more, he'll have a princess in a golden dress right here at home…(*Starts pulling her golden dress onto ALISA.*)

You're beautiful, you've no idea how beautiful you are, you're as beautiful as death…No! More beautiful than I ever was. Oh, Vladimir knows how to be so kind and gentle, you'll see, you'll see how he'll love you…

I always wanted a child like you. A little golden girl exactly like you. Alice. I'm going to call you Alice, because you came here to me, to us, to our wonderful country, to save me. Alice, I think Vladimir's going to like this. We'll never be alone again, there'll be the three of us now, you'll be with us for ever. We'll be a proper family.

You're beautiful like Alice, Alice from Wonderland…My golden Alice from Wonderland…(*As she dresses her, she drags her to the table and leans her back on a chair. Talking to her the whole time.*)

First we're going to pray. I'll do it instead of you, you just listen, no, you repeat quietly after me…

Lord God, our Father, who art in heaven, who art the only light of this world, take pity on me, take pity on my wounded soul and on my injured heart, which turns to you in the most dreadful torment with only one supplication. You did not grant me the child I asked you for in vain for so many years. You gathered him to you even before I could give birth to him. Only you know how much I suffered, how many tears I shed over him. And the moment time had healed the last wound of bitter memory, when I was dried up with weeping, you put this girl in my way, this golden girl, to ease my loneliness.

Take pity on me, you who in your infinite benevolence presented her to me, don't grant her, don't allow her to go away from me. Don't take away today what you gave me yesterday!

There! You're so beautiful!

And now go ahead and eat, so you'll get strong! You must be strong, or you won't survive. You'll get used to it, don't be afraid of anything, people can get used to anything. How do you think I did? Some men somehow think we women came into the world with a broom. Vladimir does, God help him!

Just taste a little, go on. You cooked it really well, it's very good. You could make an excellent housewife…(*Eats, bringing it to her lips very slowly and talking very fast, more or less without pause.*)

He'll come tomorrow, I know he will, I feel it, I've not been wrong yet. And how surprised he'll be, poor thing, when he sees what I've prepared for him. I can just see his face all contrite, standing at the door and looking at the floor, because he's too ashamed to look me in the face. He's ashamed, the coward, because he's dirty. First I'll send him to the bathroom, to wash off the filth. Then I'll prepare breakfast, or rather you will, and then his big confession will start. Always the same old story! I know it word for word already, inside out and back to front. I'm not worth enough to him for him to even bother to think up something new! Why should he? If I've always forgiven him…But now? How surprised he'll be, poor thing, he never expected anything like this even in his wildest dreams. Be a good girl and eat up. Yes, that's right. If you're good, you'll get a reward…(*Laughs.*) And Vladimir will get a lovely reward too, if he's good. You'll have to obey everything he says, because he's going to be your father now. Understand? Do you understand? Are you listening? Listen to me, if you don't I'll…! (*Bangs on the table.*) I can't stand spoiled children, do you hear?

There, we've eaten, now we can go to bed! I'll do the clearing up…(*Begins to pile up the dishes. Then she holds ALISA and kisses her, presses her to her, weeps. When she releases her, ALISA's body collapses lifeless.*)

Are you full up? What's the matter with you, Alice? Why don't you answer? Look at me, look at me! Go on, get up. Vladimir won't do anything to you, he won't, do you hear, you must know he wouldn't…now you're my, our daughter…Look at me, look at me, if I tell you! Alisa? Stop doing this to me! (*Hits ALISA.*) Don't mess me about, Alisa…Alisa, Alisa! (*Kisses her again and holds her.*) Alisa, my Alisa…

(*Suddenly gets up and runs to look in ALISA'S dress lying on the floor. A notebook and the empty bottle of her tranquilisers fall out. She cries out and throws the pill bottle against the wall, so that the glass breaks. Then she staggers around the room, and pours out the last drops of liquid from the bottle of cognac.*)

(*The room fills with quiet music. The motif is reminiscent of the country ALISA ran away from to us.*)

(*Darkness slowly descends. The music blares. Silence.*)

(*A ray of light. The lights come up slowly, a different quality of light. Morning. Everything on stage is as it was. MAGDA is lying on the floor next to ALISA's corpse, which is wrapped in a white sheet. The telephone rings. MAGDA embraces ALISA. It rings for a long time. Then it stops, and there is silence. The telephone rings again, and MAGDA gets up. She is tired, and is still wearing the same clothes. She drags herself to the telephone, and at the last moment lifts the receiver.*)

MAGDA
How do you mean, did I survive…? Leo, is that you? Hey…! (*The person on the other end of the phone has apparently hung up.*)
How dare you! You shit! Lousy git…

(She sits down, and stares at ALISA'S corpse. Shortly afterwards the outside buzzer rings: a short buzz, then once again. In a panic, MAGDA starts to drag ALISA'S corpse over to the bedroom door. The sound of someone approaching can be heard from the hallway. MAGDA has almost managed to get the corpse into the bedroom. Just as she is closing the bedroom door, the front door opens. VLADIMIR enters. ALISA'S leg is sticking out through the bedroom door. MAGDA stands still, as does VLADIMIR. They look at each other for a long time).

VLADIMIR
Well – how are you doing?

MAGDA
Good morning.

VLADIMIR
Yes, sorry – Good…Are you on your way out?

MAGDA
No, I've just…come back…

VLADIMIR
I thought…I haven't come for my things, you know…(*Laughing.*) Is this when I'm supposed to get down on my knees and crawl, then…?

MAGDA
That's the last thing I want you to do!

VLADIMIR
Oh, thanks. I thought so.

(MAGDA does not respond. VLADIMIR sits down.)

MAGDA
Insects crawl.

VLADIMIR
Oh, yes, all over the place. Is it all right…I mean all right with you, if…?

MAGDA
It's Sunday.

VLADIMIR
Oh, yes,…Oh, I see! What an idiot! Sorry. (*Hits himself on the head as though*

he has remembered. After a pause.) Have you had a visitor?

MAGDA
That too. Now eat at last.

VLADIMIR
I'm not hungry. Who was it?

MAGDA
Eat it up!

VLADIMIR
It's very kind of you, but I really can't. You know what I usually eat for breakfast!

(*MAGDA piles the food onto his plate*.)

MAGDA
Usually…! Why didn't you call to say you were coming for breakfast?

VLADIMIR
What are you getting angry for now?

MAGDA
Smell it, maybe you'll like it. I know it was cooked six months ago, but it's still basically fresh. You just warm it up a bit every day, add a bit of salt…and you don't even notice…

VLADIMIR
Look, it takes two to fight. Every time I've stepped through this door, you've attacked me. I haven't been able to get a thing right.

(*MAGDA laughs*.)
I know you've got your own version. But…I could apologise, but it wouldn't make you any better. You're going to have to take a long look at yourself, if you don't want to be…

MAGDA
(*Looks at her hands*.) Clean and disciplined to the end of my days. Do you see any signs of ageing? Depends on your taste. You won't know till you've tried.

VLADIMIR
Nice to see you joking, but…There's something you've got to understand…Oh, all right, I'll just have a little. (*Begins to eat*.)

MAGDA
(*Watches him carefully*.) You haven't washed your hands today.

VLADIMIR
(*Laughs*.) Yes, I did, otherwise how would I dare to enter your kingdom? Who did you say had been here?

MAGDA
That tie's had it.

VLADIMIR
You could at least buy me another one. I wouldn't mind if you bought two or three.

MAGDA
Things go out of fashion quickly, then they're forgotten.

VLADIMIR
Yes, and that's how it should be. You can't keep dragging out – I mean, keep on wearing – the same old things.

MAGDA
No. But you can keep on doing the same shit in the same old way.

VLADIMIR
It was very nice, but…(*Puts down the cutlery*.)

MAGDA
(*Picks up the chrysanthemums from the table and starts to rip up the leaves*.)
You must eat it all. Perhaps she's overcooked it a little…?

VLADIMIR
No, it's just right. Even now it's cold it's still tasty…Didn't you cook it yourself?

MAGDA
I never have done.

VLADIMIR
What? What are you shredding those for?

MAGDA
I've never done anything without lovely thoughts of you.

VLADIMIR
That's really nice. But they're not marguerites.

MAGDA
You don't say!! Well done. These aren't marguerites. They're not marguerites! Well, what if they were? What if they're just that – marguerites? Red marguerites, listen to me, not white, red! Even if objectively speaking they're not. As long as they are to me, what does it matter? You came back so you could start trying to teach me again, point out what I've dropped off the table, so…so you can tell me what you think I can see, what I hear, what I'm holding in my hands! (*She picks up even more flowers and tears them into pieces.*)

VLADIMIR
I understand why you'd be angry, but…There's really no point in quarrelling and concerning ourselves with the past all our lives. As long as we can forget what's happened, I mean what went wrong between us…put it behind us, then we can move on. We both know it won't work any other way, there wouldn't be any point.

MAGDA
No point?! He can talk to me about point?! About the point of living? Go on, swallow this for afters! (*Throws the flowers onto his plate.*) Eat up! Maybe you'll get diarrhoea and you won't have to go to her funeral. That's what you'd like, isn't it? Fucking coward.

VLADIMIR
You bitch. Are you trying to tell me…?! (*Raises his hand, reconsiders; a long silence.*) Couldn't you be a little more specific for the sake of mutual understanding? First of all, can you stick with some basic rules of behaviour? I've no idea what you're trying to say with that shit. What has she got to do with what's between us? Could you explain that to me, please?! What's she got to do with it, if…? If it's been this way ever since I've known you…Ugh!

MAGDA
Yes. I've never wanted to look at all of you. I was afraid of your mouth, I could only touch it sometimes when it was quiet. It was always red-hot. Your saliva put out the fire. Oh, do you remember?

Yes. You're right again. That's why you became my teacher. Only without my permission. Well, now I'd like to pay you back so I won't be in your debt.

VLADIMIR
You idiot, what did I bother to come for?!

MAGDA
Maybe you were interested in my arse as well?

(*A long silence; they stare into space.*)

VLADIMIR
I'm going. You're right, there's no point. It was too...I'm off...Have fun.

(*VLADIMIR starts towards the front door. At that moment he notices ALISA, who is lying in the bedroom doorway. He goes over to the door and opens it. He is horrified.*)

MAGDA
She's drunk too much again. What can you do.

VLADIMIR
Who? I mean...what's her...?

MAGDA
Alisa, Alice...Alice is only her working name.

(*The stage picture freezes for a moment. The lights go down quickly.*)

THE END

Translator's Afterword

Alisa, Alice is about xenophobia. It is also about Europe's official policy towards refugees, since the subtextual dialogue of the play is between Europe and Bosnia. In the author's opinion, we do not have the right to construct plays about Bosnia or any other suffering nation to which we do not belong. This view has led her to set the play's action, which occurs in the context of the Bosnian war, not in Bosnia itself but in a bourgeois apartment in Slovenia.

Slovenia is the northernmost country of the former federation of Yugoslavia. Bordered by Austria to the north, Italy to the west, Hungary to the east, and Croatia to the south, it is situated at the crossroads of three European linguistic and cultural systems: the Slavic, the Germanic and the Latin. The population includes immigrants from all the countries of the former Yugoslavia, a result of the policy of worker migration under the former Yugoslavian regime. Although the primary cultural influences Slovenes like to respond to are from the north and west, influences from the east are intrinsic, resulting in an unusual and interesting cultural mix.

In 1991, after a ten-day war in which there were few casualties, Slovenia achieved independence for the first time in a thousand years. Slovenia is termed a 'Second World' country, that is, one of those countries which abandoned socialism in the eighties and nineties and, having embraced parliamentary democracy, are now trying to deal with the experience of 'post socialism.'

Slovenia today is no longer closed in on itself as it was when it was part of the old Austria under the Hapsburgs, nor even as it was later as part of the former Yugoslavia. Since 1991, the terms 'Slovenian art' and 'Slovenian theatre' have begun to appear in an international context for the first time, even though these concepts have been familiar to Slovenes for a thousand years. Unfamiliar with the federal system of former Yugoslavia, most other Europeans have subsumed Slovenian theatre into what used to be thought of as 'Yugoslavian theatre.' As a result, Slovenia remains, as critic Jana Pavlič has remarked, one of the great unknowns of the European theatre movement.[1]

In the eighties, the audience for Slovenian theatre had included those who attended the major festivals in different parts of the former Yugoslavia, where the official language was Serbo-Croatian.[2] However, Slovenian, Croatian, Serbian, Bosnian and Macedonian audiences were able to understand each other's languages well enough to follow plays performed in each other's languages (more so than potential audiences from other Slavic countries). When the Bosnian war began in 1992, these festivals became increasingly rare, and the audience for Slovenian theatre productions shrank considerably.

Contemporary dance groups and young experimental theatre companies, less language-bound than dramatic theatre, were able to find new festival audiences in Europe and South America, but playwrights became increasingly dependent on translation and print to reach an audience outside their own country. The difficulty was increased by a decline in the number of cultural magazines, particularly those which had published plays, and by a shift in focus from producing plays for artistic reasons to selling them for economic survival.

Slovenia's large institutional state repertory companies are based in a few regional centres: the capital Ljubljana in the centre; Celje in the east; Kranj to the north; Maribor in the north-east and Nova Gorica in the west on the Italian border, as well as the Slovenian Theatre of Trieste (Trst in Slovene) which is funded by the Italian government. After 1991, new commercial theatre companies began to develop and travelled to other Slovenian towns. The large institutional companies have survived, as they continue to be almost entirely state-funded in the traditional way. Though they still keep plays in their repertoires for five years, commercial competition has begun to limit their freedom to offer more experimental and innovative work. This conservative influence, for example, has tended to encourage a continued basing of their work on the familiar principles of Stanislavsky. A significant exception to this rule has been the Mladinsko Theatre, whose actors and young directors follow many different paths of exploration, research and innovative performance.

Slovenian theatrical production in the nineteen-fifties and -sixties, like that in the rest of Yugoslavia, was strongly influenced by existentialist and absurdist plays, mainly from France. Fortunately there were no banned authors at the time, and traditional socialist realism and conservative social drama were increasingly replaced by a new Slovenian drama, responding to the influences from abroad. The recognition of a different kind of dramaturgy, as found in such plays as Ionesco's *The Lesson*, in turn stimulated a new kind of acting. A small group of playwrights, critics and directors – as well as a few individuals who combined these functions – whose views were sometimes politically controversial, worked together to explore the new dramaturgical possibilities.

Other influences also began to be felt, such as those from the Polish avant-garde and the anthropologically oriented work of Richard Schechner's Performance Group in New York. The latter was imported by Lado Kralj, now Professor of Comparative Literature at the University of Ljubljana, who studied with Schechner and participated in some of his group's performances.

The German tradition of politically committed theatre also had an impact. In the nineteen-eighties, political dissidence became an important element in the Slovenian theatre, particularly in the capital Ljubljana, which had been known as the last station on the Moscow metro. This small provincial city became a capital of alternative culture, the site of an eternal revolution 'fighting…for the rights of all the unknown, humiliated and offended'.[3] The Mladinsko Theatre, of which Dragica Potočnjak was a member, became a leading theatre in the eighties, serving as a crucible for the revolutionary investigation of previously taboo subjects. This company explored working methods and aesthetics in order to clarify as yet undefined processes, at the same time as giving expression to social tensions, while the authorities looked away. The young directors and writers working together on such experimentation were all trained at Slovenia's only theatre school, the Academy of Theatre, Radio, Film and Television, which was also the only conservatoire for actors. Towards the end of the decade, however, the close relationship between playwrights and directors broke up, as some of the most important writers became more directly involved in politics. At the same time as these developments, the aesthetics of theatre was also changing towards more visually oriented work, focusing on body movement, visual aesthetics, conceptual art and technology, representing a link back to the early twentieth-century Russian avant-garde. During the eighties, then, some Slovenian theatre, whether textually or visually oriented, remained highly aesthetic and experimental and generated a strong audience response.

When independence came in the nineties, a more liberal society was created with the change from a one party system to a parliamentary democracy. The theatre had the task of becoming acquainted with this new society and the new taboos it may have brought with it to replace the old ones of ideology or political party. Only then would it be possible to react critically and constructively to the changes which were taking place. Much of the discussion of this time revolved around why there was no longer any 'political theatre,' why the issues of contemporary society were no longer the essential focus of new playwriting and how these new societal problems could be treated within the theatre. Should they be dealt with in new playwriting by exploring the reverberations of the Bosnian war, or perhaps by discovering contemporary realities in classic texts (as for example Emil Filipčič's adaptation of Moliere's *Tartuffe* in which the leading character was made the head of a market dealing in human body parts)? The decision for playwrights was made even more difficult by the fact that the audiences – who in the eighties had reacted so strongly and positively to political theatre – had now given way to those who did not want to see plays written directly about the wars in the neighbouring countries of the Balkans.[4] An extreme reaction to the dilemma faced by playwrights was seen in the retreat of one thirty-five-year-old director from the theatre in order to work towards completing his performance in the year 2045, when he would be catapulted into the cosmos! His gesture perhaps marked a withdrawal by many to an inner life away from the unthinking savagery of a neo-liberal society engaged primarily in the struggle for profit. The almost pathological narcissism of this society has, in the view of some writers, caused it to distance itself from any art with meaning and significance, often focusing instead on image without intellectual content. The general refusal of the theatre-going public to assume responsibility is one consequence of the policies and actions of the former regime, which allowed little possibility of public intervention. The dispersal of any clear object of rebellion and the fading interest in theatre as an effective instrument for social change have contributed to the alarming fact that there are today hardly any playwrights below the age of thirty-five.

In 1992, Dragica Potočnjak founded a theatre group, 'The Incorrigible Optimists,' made up of young Bosnian refugees, with whom she continued until 1996. For her work with them as playwright, director, and producer, she was awarded the Europe Prize in Tampere, Finland, in 1994. She has worked as an actress since 1981 in the highly regarded experimental Mladinsko Theatre, where she took an active part in the theatricalization of contemporary texts. This experience in a theatre that was a leading force in theatrical innovation in Slovenia, has contributed importantly to her remarkable achievements as a writer. To move constantly between the writing desk and the stage takes formidable energy and is a more unusual route than the usual transfer of actors into directing. A successful playwright since 1991, she has had all her plays staged by major theatres in Slovenia, including the National Theatre. She is a person of remarkable integrity, outspoken and with a keen sense of justice, qualities which have occasionally had a negative effect on her theatrical career in a world where it is already difficult to succeed as a female playwright. In 1992 she was the first woman to be nominated for the Grum award for the best Slovenian playwright of the year in all the thirty-five years that this award has existed. Since that time she has been nominated for each of her plays.[5]

Dragica Potočnjak's active stage experience at the Mladinsko Theatre involved her with the work of a variety of Slovenian authors. The current artistic director of the theatre, Tomaž Toporišič, indicates some of those with whom she shares certain similarities of outlook or style.[6] For example, in *Alisa, Alice* we find a tone not unlike Dominik Smole's world of absurd intimate relations and Rudi Šeligo's banal grotesqueries of contemporary life. We are reminded too of Dušan Jovanović's almost absurdist approach to realism and Danilo Kiš's problematization of post-revolutionary woman. The use of language in *Alisa, Alice* shows a virtuosity not unlike that of Milan Jesih, while the cultural and religious clash of the two main characters, Magda and Alisa, is reminiscent of the grotesque world of Emil Filipčič's plays. Ivo Svetina's intertextual reinterpretations of fairy tales are echoed in the mirroring of *Alice in Wonderland*. The opposition of Alisa and Magda in this play may also be seen as bearing a structural similarity to Jovanović's *The Puzzle of Courage*,[7] in which he juxtaposes two women: the first a Bosnian woman (a variant of Brecht's model), who courageously overcomes the fate imposed by her surroundings; the second a Slovenian actress struggling to relate to Brecht's character on the stage. For all of the echoes of other characteristics to be found in *Alisa, Alice*, however, it is the individual soul – whether Muslim or Christian, weakened by pain or demoralized by suffering – that holds central sway in the play's action.

While the world engages in collective amnesia, Dragica Potočnjak tries to restore morality to the stage. For her, writing plays means having a moral connection and responsibility to the times we live in; she feels no affinity with art that inclines towards nihilism. She also seeks to contribute to the redressing of gender imbalance. As long as it remains harder for women to achieve so many important things in life, she will write predominantly for them. Writing in freedom after the Slovenian Independence of 1991, she did not fall victim to the 'unbearable lightness' of the artistic freedom of the time.[8] Her research has been not merely into the theatrical and the performative, but also to find ways of establishing through her writing values that barely exist in the present crisis of ethics, while at the same time revealing the moral manipulations that do. For her, words are urgently connected with responsibility. Socially engaged, she wants to get away from a theatre occupied with contemplating its own navel. Merely describing the state of affairs in the world is not enough for an artistic work; it must also engage with them. Tomaž Toporišič has questioned what kind of discourse is appropriate today, after the nineteen-nineties, which embodied the final phase of the hegemony of heterogeneity (the heritage of the post-modernism of the eighties) in a politics committed to global unification.[9] In the middle of October 1991, just before the fall of Vukovar, Dragica Potočnjak wrote a letter, signed by almost everyone in her theatre, to theatres and cultural institutions in Serbia, appealing to them to take sides against the appalling butchery and slaughter that was taking place in the name of their people. She received not a single reply.[10]

Cultural exchange used to be a part of communist doctrine in the former Yugoslavia, and Slovenian playwrights benefited from open dialogue with their south-eastern neighbours in Croatia, Serbia and Bosnia.[11] Finally, in 2001, after years of separation, the Slovenian National Theatre visited Belgrade, receiving an overwhelmingly positive response, even from those who had never been to the theatre before. Past differences had been put aside and in 2002 the visit was reciprocated.

In her first play *Blind Mice* (1991), and in her second *The Dance of a Butterfly* (1992) (performed to sold-out houses at the Slovenian National Theatre) Dragica Potočnjak depicts a human condition described by the philosopher Tine Hribar in an essay on *Butterfly* as one in which we question: 'Why we live at all when life as life is no longer enough. When we begin to doubt in…ourselves. When we feel in ourselves an unbearable lack. A hole that cannot be filled. We are facing a state of dissatisfaction. This dissatisfaction is

77

not only a possible professional one, but also a sexual and erotic one, and above all an existential dissatisfaction. A dissatisfaction that cannot be equated with Lacanian desire'.[12] In *Alisa, Alice*, Magda embodies this dissatisfaction. An example of the type is described by the theatre historian Taras Kermauner: it 'can express its inner self only by means of perverted human relations, sadomasochism, the destruction of the other, forcing this other finally into death; the torturer either killing him [sic] or the tortured committing suicide'.[13] Magda, through the sadism arising from her despair and loss of purpose, her psychological confusion, causes the suicide of the young refugee Alisa. In places, the style of the play is reminiscent of Pinter's comedy of menace. According to Toporišič, the liberal Western values of 'private happiness, pleasure, social success, image' are enclosed in the hot-houses of the petty bourgeoisie, 'small, breathless spaces, in which there is a lack of open communication and spontaneity', where the inhabitants remain unsatisfied and unable to satisfy others.[14]

While *Blind Mice* and *Butterfly Dance* depict this dissatisfaction through the interpersonal relations of the Western bourgeois family, *Alisa, Alice* (1997) goes on to describe the impossibility of understanding between two very different cultures. The first is represented by a young refugee woman from 'tribal' Bosnia, the second by a middle-aged Slovenian woman from Western liberal society. Her next play, *Kalea* (1999) is sub-titled 'a social drama with a gypsy theme', and deals with the social conditions within contemporary society of cultural and national minorities, showing how a so-called 'tribal' society loses its balance and begins to disintegrate. *Empty Shoes* (2001) is a 'fictional drama based on a real event' which begins with war (in this case the Bosnian war) and then describes post-war society through the struggle of a mentally handicapped boy and his grandmother.

These plays are all concerned with exposing the decay of ethics in two societies, the liberal Western petty bourgeoisie of the European Union and the 'tribal', ethnic, Balkan states of the former Yugoslavia. Taras Kermauner reads *Alisa, Alice* with the following gloss: 'In Bosnia (Bosnia being the symbolic name for the kind of society referred to) the representatives of different nations are slaughtering each other, burning down each other's houses, as if highly civilised Italians did not do this during the Second World War in Slovenia; they are destroying and devastating entire villages, as if the Russians are not doing exactly the same thing with Chechenia; they are raping, note the Thirty Years War in Europe between highly developed Catholics and Protestants; they are physically torturing each other, as if the highly developed Romans did not do the same thing to the Christians...'[15]

When people kill each other, there is no escape from the psychic confusion that has caused such action. According to Taras Kermauner, Magda is a victim of a post-modern middle-class liberal society in which all values that do not concern personal happiness, pleasure, social success and image (represented by Irena and Leo in the play) have disappeared, all routes to any kind of transcendence have been blocked, meaningful communication has been stifled. Contemporary Slovenian plays, following the prevailing Western Zeitgeist, are telling us this all the time. Dragica Potočnjak shows that such values can only lead to interpersonal torture and destruction. Magda's hopes turn into memories; on the edge of hysteria, she tries to blame others in order to find a way out of her situation. She is as much a victim of her kind of society as Alisa is of hers. To extricate herself from this world, Magda would need either a religion or an inner world that her surroundings cannot help her to find. Her soul, like her world, is concerned with material comfort and superficial values. From a social perspective, however, Magda has more opportunities and more freedom than Alisa, and is therefore seen to be more guilty. As an exponent of Slovenian provincial thinking, she is criticised far more in the play than Alisa, with whom our sympathies lie. But we would do well, the playwright is saying, to pay attention to her predicament.

Taras Kermauner has pointed out that in Slovenia refugees are not merely refugees, but part of Slovenian reality. It is, of course, far harder for refugees to live in their new surroundings than for those already there. To survive, they must live intensively, make extraordinary efforts to engage, open their eyes and ears more widely than before, watch out for themselves more carefully, stand their ground more firmly. They must live with minds full of powerful memories. In the most difficult moments of their vigorous fight for survival, a part of themselves will always float away into their memories, their only true home. These are not memories of a nation, but of a home, a village. According to Dragica Potočnjak, those, like Magda, who are relatively well off in the world, experience an almost hysterical fear when confronted with the misery and poverty of such people. They also have the inner conviction that they have more right to live than these others do. During the Bosnian war, approximately thirty thousand refugees were incarcerated in Slovenian camps for three months before they were released.[16] At the same time, European and other foreign advisors, though their faces may have been sour, still shook the hand of Milošević. For reasons like these, for Dragica Potočnjak the word 'humanitarian' sounds like a slap in the face, the self-righteous phrase 'human rights' has become the greatest lie on earth.

In her five years of work with Bosnian refugees, Dragica Potočnjak acted as a medium or conductor through which the participants of the theatrical and writing workshops could give form to their experiences and convey them to others. Only those who have themselves come through war, she believes, have the right to speak in artistic form of the horrific experiences they have been through. The outside artist observing a war blasphemes if s/he usurps the right to speak from a position on the inside. The texts she wrote were created together with the refugees in these workshops. At the same time, attempting to write of the 'truth' of war seems to her nonsensical, for no word can be bloodier than blood, or hurt as much as a real wound. For her this has been particularly so since the decline in the power of the word throughout the twentieth century that Czeslaw Milosz describes in his essay 'The Immorality of Art'.[17] This deterioration of the word continues, she believes, in an accelerating avalanche, carrying away more and more words and even languages.

Alisa, Alice, written between 1994 and 1997, was begun whilst the war was still going on. Dragica Potočnjak chose to write the play from a distance, from a position amongst the observers of the war, finding a story that would talk about the war's consequences yet speak to, and take place, in a comfortable Europe. Politics as such are not mentioned in the play; here the personal is political. The personification that occurs in the representation is not Alisa as Bosnia, but rather the relationship between Magda and Alisa, symbolizing the attitudes and behaviour of Europe and the rest of the world to Bosnia. Language and communication are in *Alisa, Alice* symbolic of a lack of real dialogue in life and are themselves a site of conflict. In particular, the play represents how heavily Bosnia had to pay for the paucity of the dialogue between itself and the rest of Europe. When Bosnia called out for help, while the people and children of Srebrenica were dying of hunger in the streets like abandoned dogs, Europe debated. Alisa dies because she has lost her belief in life. She could have assimilated into the Slovenian culture, spoken excellent Slovene after a few years, got a job, perhaps married a Slovene, but she had been too deeply wounded to want these things. She would have needed someone to help her, just as they might help someone seriously ill. But Magda is preoccupied with her own pain, again reflecting a common reason for the undermining of humanitarian impulses. As a result of such self-preoccupation on a grand scale, when Serbian military butchers killed tens of thousands of innocent people, including children, the self-proclaimed guardians of human rights gave them free rein. Then these same people moralised to the victims' surviving relatives about tolerance and peaceful coexistence between nations. Despite all this, however, the author offers a note of optimism at the end of the play. Magda, at least, has recognised her mistakes.[18] Now we see coming out of the war crime trials at the Hague some slight recognition of a similar kind.

Endnotes

1   Jana Pavlič, 'De la discothèque rose au théâtre en apesanteur,' *Alternatives Théâtrales* 64. (2000): 49, my translation.

2   A Slovene in the Yugoslav army who refused to speak Serbo-Croatian would be classified as illiterate on their identity card. In *Alisa, Alice* inverted echoes of this can be heard in Magda's insistence on the use of Slovene by Alisa.

3   Jana Pavlič, 'De la discothèque rose au théâtre en apesanteur,' *Alternatives Théâtrales* 64. (2000): 49, my translation.

4   Tomaž Toporišič, Artistic Director of the Mladinsko Theatre, Ljubljana, personal interview, 27 April 2002.

5   In 2001, Maja Weiss became the first woman in Slovenia to make a full-length film.

6   Tomaž Toporišič, 'Draga Potočnjak y el teatro esloveno actual: Desvelando el vacío ético en la sociedada moderna,' *Primer Acto, Cuadernos de Investigación Teatral* 2. 288 (2001): 33-37.

7   Dušan Jovanovič, *The Puzzle of Courage*, trans. Lesley Wade Soule. In *Litterae Slovenicae: Contemporary Slovenian Drama*, 35.90 (1997): 151-91.

8   From the title of *The Unbearable Lightness of Being* by the Czech exile Milan Kundera.

9   Tomaž Toporišič, 'Draga Potočnjak y el teatro esloveno actual: Desvelando el vacío ético en la sociedada moderna.' *Primer Acto, Cuadernos de Investigación Teatral*. 2. 288 (2001): 33-37.

10   Dragica Potočnjak, Slovensko Narodno Gledališče, Repertoarni List, *Metuljev ples*. With Majda Hostnik, Ljubljana, 1996, 6, my translation.

11   Lado Kralj, personal interview, Ljubljana, 23 April, 2002.

12   Tine Hribar, Slovensko Narodno Gledališče, Repertoarni List, *Metuljev ples*. Ljubljana, 1996, 10.

13   Taras Kermauner, 'Točna diagnoza: človek v pasti,' Slovensko Ljudsko Gledališče Celje, Repertoarni List, *Alisa, Alica*. Celje, December 1999.

14   Tomaž Toporišič, 'Draga Potočnjak y el teatro esloveno actual: Desvelando el vacío ético en la sociedada moderna,' *Primer Acto, Cuadernos de Investigación Teatral*, 2. 288 (2001): 33-37.

15   Taras Kermauner, 'Točna diagnoza: človek v pasti,' Slovensko Ljudsko Gledališče Celje, Repertoarni List, *Alisa, Alica*. Celje, December 1999.

16   Dragica Potočnjak, personal interview, Ljubljana, 24 April, 2002.

17   Czeslaw Milosz, 'The Immorality of Art'. In *Vrt Ved*, Krakov: Ogrod nauk, 1979.

18   Dragica Potočnjak, *Sodobnost* 5.1, 2000. With Petra Pogorevec.